Bread and **Butter:**

A SELF-DIRECTED DISCOVERY TO YOUR DESIRED LIFE

Deborah Liverett

BALBOA
PRESS
A DIVISION OF HAY HOUSE

Balboa Press books may be ordered through booksellers or by contacting:

Balboa Press
A Division of Hay House
1663 Liberty Drive
Bloomington, IN 47403
www.balboapress.com
1-(877) 407-4847

Printed in the United States of America

ISBN: 978-1-4525-6806-5 (sc)
ISBN: 978-1-4525-6808-9 (hc)
ISBN: 978-1-4525-6807-2 (e)

Library of Congress Control Number: 2013902165

Balboa Press rev. date: 10/29/2014

Dedications

Mommy, thanks for nurturing me.

Aunt Pat, thanks for editing and for every encouraging word along the way.

R.J., Justin and my daughters-in-love, thanks for being my champions.

Family, thanks for loving me.

Friends, thank you for believing I could. Angela and Kismet, thanks for the early and consistent support. Connie, you are the very best at holding me up in the light.

To my clients, thank you for sharing your lives, fears and hopes with me. You have helped me to continue to examine my own life based on your lessons.

To my ego (which is extremely upset), thank you for wanting to protect me.

Table of Contents

Preface

*B*READ AND *B*UTTER DEVELOPED out of a critical cry from people grappling to understand why their lives don't resemble their hopeful desires. This is a self-discovery book that encourages readers to examine their beliefs, their lives, their choices, and their responsibilities to change. *Bread and Butter* is a metaphor for a great life. Many people merely exist from day to day; they are complacent with the bread of life. As they define and choose their ideal life, they begin experiencing the bread and butter that the Universe has to offer. Savory, earthy bread and creamy butter are birthrights of each of us.

People who pretend all is well while wondering secretly, *Is this all there is?* will benefit from reading *Bread and Butter*. For all of us who are experiencing increasing demands on our lives, challenging job markets, and our propensity to be outcome-driven, but who are unable to create any real change, the practical themes and questions in this book will prove beneficial. When people are willing to devote time, attention, and focus to the task of changing, they begin to embrace an enhanced quality of life with relationships at home and work.

Often adults who have experienced childhood trauma that was not addressed or discussed (and who among us hasn't?) are walking wounded. Many people have desires, yet their lives go in directions contrary to those directions. They say to me, "Duty calls," or their idea of current responsibilities trumps all personal desires. People actually believe they do not have a right to personal happiness or fulfillment. They begin to lose sight of who they are or feel inside themselves, like a house divided.

I have heard numerous adults say that they don't know what their passion is or who they are any more. This book is designed to help people define their own journey, and it does so by presenting ancient beliefs through practical and modern examples. It helps you to get to know whom you chose to be.

Most self-help books instruct their readers on a number of personal problems, with a focus on popular psychology, blocking emotional impulse (have you heard of "fake it until you make it"?), and self-control. My focus is self-creation through personal choice. *Bread and Butter* is a personal journey that explores how I found and ultimately revealed who I am, how I try to make a difference in the world, and the questions that have helped me (and many of my clients) determine our own ideas of satisfaction. This book is a replication of the work that I do with satisfied clients. Don't expect every question to resonate with you. Do try to answer by kneading deeply to uncover your core beliefs; be open to new ideas that will get you to your dream life complete with fulfillment and internal, long-lasting joy. Most of us are not taught how to create lives of pure joy and purpose. We are often led to do what others think are the right things for us. One day we wake up feeling old and tired and can't place a finger on why. Other people might be right about your life's purpose, but how can you know if you don't examine it for yourself? If your answer to why you believe something is because your parent, minister, or teacher told you, I would like to challenge you to examine the premise for your own answer. It may well be the same answer; the point is to know it for yourself. If the answers don't resonate within you, it is difficult to ever have your own voice in your life.

As far as we know, an unexamined life is a series of events that lead us around. We blame other people for what is wrong in our lives. We complain and expect things will change without any effort on our parts. Nothing changes without internal work. People move to another location only to find they have taken themselves along. People date and marry the same types of people without understanding that the common denominator is self. That is why this book suggests living through awareness and conscious choice. Examine where you began, heal the hurts, and forgive the disappointments and traumas to live fully free and to see clearly what is happening in front of you. There is no greater journey than this pathway, because, dear reader, this is your life, and therefore it's your choice.

Bread and Butter:

A Self-Directed Discovery to Your Desired Life

Introduction

L IFE GIVES US GIFTS, and one of mine was packaged as my fifth grade teacher, Mrs. Bean. She was paid to impart knowledge, but I doubt that she had any way of knowing that the wisdom of her words would serve me throughout my life. She bent from her waist over my desk at Marcus Hook Elementary School; her acute observation was whispered in my ear so the other children couldn't hear: "With a little effort, you can have the bread and butter, but you choose to be satisfied with only the bread." She wasn't referring to my lunchroom eating habits. Mrs. Bean, literally the tallest woman in my life, cared enough to push me to want to apply my mind toward getting the best grades with a modest increase of personal effort. I am grateful that those words stay with me, encouraging me to do better and to extend myself beyond my first thought of what I can do.

This book is my attempt at sharing the philosophy of a bread-and-butter life. It's about achieving the very best that is in you by actualizing your soul's reason for being on earth. Thank you, Mrs. Bean, wherever you are. Thanks also to all true teachers worldwide—those who believe in their students' abilities to grow and be of service to themselves and the world.

Spiritual Journey

*Personal growth begins when self-examination
becomes a necessity for change.*

I CHOSE TO START A quest for meaning and self-discovery with a spiritual journey rather than a specific religious ideology. I studied many religions and have very clear ideas about what works for me based on study and reflection. The two merge at times, but I set myself on a course of understanding what was right for me. I encourage you to understand what is your internal *Source* and how it impacts your daily life.

How do you depend on your Source?

How does your Source support you?

Are you part of your Source, or do you exist outside of it?

These answers become your foundation for support and growth on your way to having bread and butter. If you can't answer these questions right away, that should not concern you. This book takes you through several series of questions within each chapter and provides lists at the end of the book. Each answer builds awareness that can help you know yourself better. As you learn more about whom you are, the once-difficult questions get easier.

My spiritual journey, which is very different from my religious upbringing, was set in motion as an adult tired of struggling against the tide of my life. From adolescence to early adulthood, I carried around a patriarchal image of God, my Supreme Parental Figure

(SPF). He could sit in His big chair from on high and survey the entire world in milliseconds. A nod of His head granted a wish for a healing miracle, or a finger pointed in your direction could take away your most loved person. My SPF could prevent a teenage pregnancy on Monday, but if one pushed her luck, maybe next Tuesday a new life would be conceived. My mental picture of God blurred between Charlton Heston as he played Moses in the 1956 movie *The Ten Commandments* and my biological father. I took my imagery seriously, thinking it was part of the connection I needed to survive. As I look back on that image, it is amusing, because before these men died, my dad was a five foot ten inch African American, and Charlton Heston was the national spokesperson for the NRA.

Is your image of your Ultimate Source any different
from your childhood deity or religious instruction?

How do you define the Ultimate Source in your life?

(Note: Use of the term *Ultimate Source* is to respect the many different names people have for the entity they believe in. When referring to my belief I will interchange the words Universe Energy (UE) and God.)

Like most children, I learned the concept of supplicative prayer at bedtime: "Now I lay me down to sleep and ask the Lord my soul to keep." Shortly after my parents' separation, when I was seven years old, I expanded the request from protection to a plea for what I came to understand to be wisdom. In my little girl mentality, if I could understand what was happening, I could ward off future pain. It was a simple prayer: "Please Lord, give me whatever it takes not to make the same mistakes twice." You see, as many children do, I thought somehow I was responsible for their breakup; if only I had been better behaved, they would have stayed together. It seemed to me that the pain from the mistake of that breakup was too intense to repeat. My survival philosophy became: "Be as good and perfect as possible—in secret hope that my SPF would grant favor over my days and nights." Twenty-seven years after my parents' separation, my own marriage failed following twelve years of me trying to be a better wife than June Cleaver. (For younger readers who may not know, June was the quintessential television wife to husband Ward and mother to sons Wally and the Beaver on *Leave It To Beaver* from 1957 to 1963.) I was spiritually and emotionally lost. I felt as if I had failed at marriage and at being a woman of wisdom. The pain that I desperately wanted to avoid was deadening. Yet the possibility of freedom to regain myself was the bright resurrection light that kept me alive.

What I learned is wisdom is not obtained by *knowing* what is right. Wisdom is gained by *practicing* what is right within your soul. Pay attention to what happens inside you when you succeed as well as when you fail. Wise people do not have to be certain about what they believe before they act. They are free to act, trusting that the practice itself will teach them what they need to know.

I came to understand that part of being an adult is examining the beliefs we were brought up on to see if they still serve us well as we live the life of our own design. If a belief is hindering your fulfillment, can you tweak that belief to serve you better? Some beliefs are big and some are small. All are meaningful enough to examine. We analyze the past to help us answer what is happening currently. It's the interpretation of life experiences that gives us insights beyond the way we were raised. Our beliefs shape our worldview and create the life we are living.

I wrestled with my old way of living because I was good at it. That way of living, however, wasn't enough to ward off heartache. What I realized was the very thing I was frightened about came into being. It was as if I had to face my fears to learn that I could survive them. I couldn't see that fact without first looking at my definition of Source. I needed to redefine my concept of God and my relationship with that God. Could these bad events help me learn new life lessons that could carry over to a life of my own design and desire? The answer turned out to be yes—for me. You can answer what it will be for you as you review the beliefs you carry today and what you decide to believe in as you go forward.

Examine your long-term beliefs about your
relationship with your Ultimate Source.

How do you rely on your Source?

Who told you what you believe?

Has your thought changed over the years?

Have your thoughts about your Source expanded or contracted?

In a deliberate way, I began examining the thoughts that were going through my head. Were the thoughts supportive of the life I wanted or in conflict with what I desired? To move beyond the old thought process, I began giving myself permission to try on new thoughts for an hour at a time. If I didn't self-destruct, I could extend the new thought into days, always giving myself permission to go back to my original perception. I began experimenting with expanded ideas about God by asking myself questions like these:

What if He isn't a punishing and rewarding figure?

What if He loves without condition?

What if our eternal souls stand by to whisper ideas of
greatness and we could choose to do something with
those ideas or not because of our Free Will?

What if all desires of the heart are God's pleasure to fulfill?

Could I be blocking my own desires?

If yes, in what ways could I be blocking my own growth and desires?

What if God's ability and grace are larger than
anyone or anything I could imagine?

Answer these questions for yourself, and more importantly, as the designer of your desired life, create some of your own questions. The ideas are yours and as personal as your relationship to your Ultimate Source.

Some people report that they are uncomfortable examining what they were taught to believe about their Ultimate Source. They believe something bad will happen. All those emotions are real. This process takes personal courage. We use courage to listen when the Universe calls upon us to do something different from what we would normally do. That courage frees us to be who we were born to be. It shows us the beauty of a life lived well and sometimes off the beaten path. Self-examination does not equal self-deterioration. Growth implies change, and self-awareness gives you an informed choice.

Through my examination, I began to see my own vision of God's support as the world's energy. Everything is energy, and it pulses continually. God's *influence* is impersonal and unparalleled. It is Universal Energy, and it is Love. Identifying God as Universal Energy reminds me that love is everywhere and in everything. I let go of my beliefs of a man in a heavenly chair with an authoritative finger pointing and punishing. If the ultimate is love, and UE loves us no matter what our own dastardly deeds, then ideally there can be no need for punishment or judgment. Man has created laws to govern our behavior. All I really needed was self-reflection and personal responsibility, because humans are capable of good and evil actions. The majority of us are not operating at either extreme but somewhere in the middle—hurting others' feelings in one minute and conducting a random act of kindness in the next.

Describe your vision of your God's support.

The notion of UE presented me with calmness and support that gave me a deep assurance that I would be all right. My thoughts tapped into a rhythm that assured my bills will get paid, my children will grow into decent people, and that I can experience joy no matter what is happening around me.

I began noticing what was happening in my life that supported my new understanding of my relationship with UE. One night three years after my divorce, I opened correspondence from my attorney. The letter stated that I had been paying fifty dollars a month, yet I still owed thousands of dollars. I cried uncontrollably. When the sobbing stopped, I thanked UE for clearing up the debt, as I knew somehow it would be. I didn't try to determine how the debt would be covered. I merely trusted it would be resolved. I continued to pay the monthly fifty-dollar allotment and affirmed that the debt was "paid in full." Approximately three months later, I received a letter explaining that my attorney had left the practice, and they were no longer going to bill me. No one ever explained why the debt was forgiven. All I know is that my understanding of the power of UE and my relationship to it created my desired result. I believed in the unbelievable without trying to figure out the details. I did the right thing, and continued to make payments. While making the payments, I aligned my belief in an energy that could move a financial mountain.

How resourceful do you view your Ultimate Source to be?

How capable is UE of creating change in your life?

Can you believe in that which you do not see currently?

*How would you describe the foundation you
want to build your true desires on?*

UE provides me with a strong and wondrous foundation. I feel my closeness with UE with gratitude in every spring breeze and Chicago winter wind. The relationship blankets me like a down comforter. The energy swirls in me, bringing to the forefront an understanding that it was my responsibility to harness my energy to create the life I desire. It is the Universe's great pleasure to give me the desires of my heart.

List a personal desire that you have been afraid or unable to actualize. For three months, practice thanking and trusting your Ultimate Source for its manifestation until it or something better materializes in your life. Thoughts contradictory to your desire have no place in your belief system. Return always to thankfulness and trustfulness.

A minister challenged her congregation to pray without ceasing, as instructed in the King James Version of the Bible. I practiced praying, but felt I failed miserably at the without ceasing part given my numerous responsibilities at the time, including working and raising children. Formal prayer all day and night just did not seem possible. To accompany my newly expanded vision of God as UE, my understanding of prayer also needed new ideas. I returned to the examination of my beliefs. I invite you to examine for yourself:

What if our thoughts are viewed as our prayers?

How would you view your thoughts if you thought of them as your prayers?

What if listening were a viable component of prayer?

How are you affected if you don't believe in the possibility of an answer to your prayers?

If you dismiss answers because of a lack of trust in yourself or the wisdom of the Ultimate Source, do you prolong the pain or unrealized desire?

I'm not suggesting we force a specific outcome or that we try to control the way we get to an outcome. We can, however, decide to accept and be grateful for any outcome when we trust its design is to teach us something spiritual about ourselves. I am grateful for all that I have and do not have in this moment: grateful for the people who didn't work out in my life, and equally grateful for meaningful current relationships and a purposeful vocation. We may not be propelled into a completely new life right away, but with each answer we can begin with small steps toward new outcomes.

So the prayer (constant affirmation) to eliminate the attorney's bill was answered and returned fifty dollars a month to my pocket. It didn't change my financial picture right away. What it did do was increase my awareness of UE's ability in my life and in the lives of others. I learned our thoughts coupled with our emotions reinforce and create life situations and solutions that teach us more about ourselves. That kind of knowledge gives us clarity and awareness of our own greatness.

Having redefined my concept of God, and seeing how my thoughts as prayers could be answered, I was ready to step boldly into my spiritual journey. How to continue the journey wasn't immediately clear to me. My uncertainty did not seem to matter, as UE was capable of divinely establishing a next step without my direct intervention or immediate awareness. It was, however, set in motion by my desire and my belief system in UE's ability to change the way things appear in our lives.

On a warm spring day, I sat in the park with a bottle of water and some fresh fruit. Intuitively, I removed my shoes to straddle my toes between the bare ground and small patches of grass. Staring at a tree full of singing birds, I began to feel my connection with the pulse of the Universe. Instinctively, I was meditating at a similar vibration as the Universe. An awareness of trees and their life cycles prompted a shift in my thought process: We don't worry when leaves begin to fall from the trees because it is understood that this release signals the automatic processing of new leaves. We also don't worry when the forming of new leaves can't immediately be seen with the naked eye. Just as in our own lives, this process of falling away of the old so that something new can emerge is rarely immediately visible. We accept that birds have branches to hang onto with or without the leaves, just as our own spiritual foundation exists with or without our awareness.

Birds raised their voices to be heard as part of the cycle. A comforting inner voice showed up and convinced me to be still and hang on long enough to find my own voice through continued meditation.

The first time I found meditation was in a yoga class during my sophomore year in college. I got special permission to take twenty-two credit hours a semester; I also worked fifteen to twenty hours a week and took an evening yoga class that introduced me to meditating on the *third eye*. Close your eyes and feel yourself lift your eyes under each eyelid so your eyes are looking up toward the middle of your forehead. The third eye is described more under chakras a few paragraphs below.

The results of the meditation were magical. I sailed through the work and class assignments with no worries or stress. The following semester I did not take the yoga and meditation class. I struggled and often vented emotionally-triggered bad-mouthing toward anyone within reach of my stressed voice. I admit it was the middle of the semester before I put together what was different and realized I wasn't regularly practicing meditation.

Another component of meditation that some people employ is the use of a mantra. Mantras help you quiet your mind. Mantras have energy. Mantras can be one word or a short, positive, uplifting statement. Concentrating on a mantra can keep you focused, which is very helpful when your mind wanders (a normal occurrence in the beginning) and you are having a hard time bringing it back to a relaxed state of being.

There are many books dedicated to the methods of meditation. I recommend you experiment with what is comfortable for you, thereby creating your own path to enlightenment. I'll explain a few of my methods merely as examples, because this book is about you figuring out what works for you.

All of my meditations begin with three deep cleansing breaths that signal my mind and body to calm down. The ritual is important to me because it presents an automatic response similar to Pavlov's experiment; my body registers the sequence of events time after time, telling my system it is time to relax. In meditation the breath is very important. The deep breaths signal the brain that it's time to return to calm. You can think of the breath *in* as peace being brought in, and the *outgoing* breath as disruptions going out. The symbolism helps your mind, organs, and being to slow down. The quiet makes a space for new thoughts, ideas, and ways to live in this world. It opens the door to new ways of coping, and it gives us clarity. It's a sacredness we all too often run from, as if being in a state of flux were normal. As you can tell from the Preface, I am a great believer in personal choice. I choose how I want to experience the day, and often it is in calmness. If flux and mayhem appeal to you, stay there, and by all means don't meditate.

I started with five minutes of focused breathing, adding five minutes with each subsequent meditation until I reached twenty to forty-five minutes, depending on how much time I had to meditate. You may find two minutes is the right place for you to start. No judgment is necessary; just do what is right for you. I breathe in and out and end grateful for feeling calm and clearheaded.

Listed below are a few meditation poses I began early on:

Corpse—Lying Down Meditation

A LYING DOWN MEDITATION starts with three deep breaths to alert UE that I intend to prepare myself for a deeper connection. I place my hands on invisible points up the middle of my body, called *chakras* by ancient Indian mystics, which are energy centers. I focus on seven chakras that each connects to our internal energy. The first chakra (known as the root) relates to our basic needs for food, shelter and safety. The root chakra is at the base of the spine. Starting at my root chakra, with my hands placed lovingly across the middle and top of my thighs, I allow myself to feel the energy flow through my hands to begin balancing the energy in the chakras. Before I move to the second chakra I wait for a sense that it is time to proceed.

This was one of the first practices that heightened my knowing and trusting in something I could not see. Like a muscle, instinctive knowing grows the more it is used.

The second chakra is associated with procreation, sexual energy, and creativity. Again, I didn't try to analyze when to move to my solar plexus (the third chakra). It represents personal power and our ability to assert ourselves appropriately.

By the time I reached the heart chakra (fourth), I noticed my breath was more relaxed than when I started. The heart chakra represents our ability to be compassionate, kind, and loving. My thoughts remained focused on breathing and trusting, while I practiced letting go of all other thoughts and concerns.

The fifth point is the throat chakra, which relates to communication and expression. I covered my eyes with my palms, allowing my fingers to touch the *third eye*, also known as the sixth chakra. This is the home of our intuition. It is there that I often see a light. It dances side to side like wheat stalks blowing in a light spring breeze, enfolded by the surrounding sun. One day the light turned into a flame and ended with sprinkles of light much like a mini firework.

Do not be discouraged if your mind races with out-of-control thoughts, or if you experience headaches, or begin to cry for no apparent reason during the first days. Let your experience unfold, and be good with it. Let go of judging what you are experiencing easily and calmly.

Lighted candles, while not necessary to meditation, are helpful to some people to help them envision the flame when their eyes are closed.

From the sixth eye chakra I moved to the top of my head, where it is believed universal knowledge awakens personal answers. This is the spiritual connection with our Ultimate Source. I continued to take deeper breaths throughout to stay focused. At the seventh chakra you are closing in on enlightenment. The outcome of aligning my chakras is that I think more clearly, and handle life's daily ups and downs more confidently.

Sitting Meditation

MY SITTING MEDITATIONS ARE a slight modification to the corpse meditation. I place my hands on my thighs, either with my palms up and open to receive external energy, or down to move internal energy through my body. My three beginning breaths remain important; they connect my brain to a quieter place within my being. Sometimes I place my hands on the chakra points, or at other times I keep my hands on my thighs. If my thinking is stuck, and the same thoughts are continually racing through my head, I may have my palms up and open to receive a message from the Universe. If I am feeling sure and ready to grow beyond where I am currently, I shift my energy by placing my palms on my thighs.

Mindful Meditation

I DO MINDFUL MEDITATIONS along with activities. For example, when I wash dishes, I stay singularly focused on the motion of my hands, the feel of dishwashing soap on my skin, and the heat from the hot water. When my mind wanders, I bring my attention back to the experience at hand. Mindful meditation allows my brain to be at peace; I can retain more information, and be less reactionary to life's mishaps. I can see each mishap as an opportunity to grow or show compassion. The benefits provide a great entry, opening the doorway to personal choice.

Mirror Meditation

WHEN MY MIND IS overloaded or I don't feel attractive or pleased with myself, I practice mirror meditation. I sit in front of a full-length floor mirror with a small candle. I follow the candle's flame until I am breathing calmly. Then I return my attention to the mirror and look into my eyes. I stay focused on my eyes until all random thoughts disappear. When I see what I imagine UE sees within me, I can feel pure love for myself, leaving behind all judgments or fears. I do not leave the mirror until I see a glimmer of divine greatness. The glimpse of inherent greatness provides the right time to for me to give thanks, to move away from the mirror and back into the world.

Meditation takes practice. You'll get to a calmer place; just remember: don't expect perfection the first weeks or months. Meditation helped to cure me of my need to be perfect. I now consider myself a recovering perfectionist; now I seek subtle changes in my reaction to life situations around me. I can quickly recognize trigger signs. For example, I know I am stressed if it upsets me when someone gets on the elevator at work with me and presses a floor before mine. How unreasonable, considering I go to the seventh floor. Through meditation I became more aware of what is bothering me. It allows me to stop reacting and start asking important questions. And I have learned to listen for the answers, which can be eye-opening and set me free to see more clearly what is in front of me.

Why am I upset?

What is stressing me?

What are various ways I can see this situation?

How can I see this situation differently and more positively?

Don't look for or expect particular outcomes with meditation. Get comfortable with just being. Nothing needs to happen. The practice opens you to receive whatever experience your energy is trying to bring to you.

Meditation reminds me that UE gives us perfect love, which does not translate into a perfect life. UE is a loving source, therefore I feel obligated to return that love to people I meet and to myself. UE is with us always. We turn toward or away from that energy.

After meditating we can appreciate when the Universe energizes us forward. Meditation opens us to new ideas and expression.

My spiritual journey is everlasting. Through meditation I was able to lay my belief of a SPF down for a larger vision. An Ultimate Source that gives me guidance.

Be aware daily of messages, guidance, hints, understandings, or dreams you receive. It's your journey with whatever source you deem best for yourself. Whether your belief is steeped in a Source greater than you, or energy vibrations, or a stronger belief in yourself—you get to decide because it's your life and your journey. You can feel your own energy as you get more in tune with your authentic self. All matter is energy—our universe that we share with millions of people and things is an infinite expression of energy that connects all living things. How you think and feel affects energy. If you feel happy, your energy expands and empowers you. But if you are feeling sad and downhearted, your energy can't support your real desires.

What are the steps you are being guided to take?

Meditation is the best form of selfishness. Consider it as part of self-reflection, which can stop cycles of negative behavior that gets in the way of successful living. It can help you avoid making the same mistakes over and over. If you repeatedly choose the wrong relationships for yourself, can't keep employment, or can't keep weight off, it's time to stop the self-sabotage and begin self-reflection instead. If you feel success is an arm's length away, self-reflection can help you check your belief system and dig deeper to question when you started feeling unworthy of the very best life has to offer. We are on earth to learn different things; however, the most meaningful lesson is love. First, we learn to love ourselves, and second, to share that love with others. Sounds simple and is simple. You merely have to contemplate deep down what you believe about yourself and this life you have been given.

Thank your Ultimate Source for providing awareness, regardless of the answers. Gratitude brings more awareness to your mind. The energy of gratitude brings you more of what you are grateful for.

It helps to write in a journal after meditation. There are times I stop meditating to write down messages I am receiving and then return to meditating. Journaling helps you see your progress. Sample questions you can start with are:

What message did I receive during meditation?

What seems different now that I've finished my meditation?

The Universe can ask us to walk into unknown territory. If you say yes, the unknown becomes a doorway. All your senses are heightened, and you are humbled because you don't know what to expect. Most of us live predictable lives. Our egos would have us believe in predictable lives, leaving us feeling safe and in control. When the ego is in charge, the authentic self is harder to hear. That's why the Universe sends us little whispers from our "real desire." The state of openness begins a shift in us. It's acceptance; it's peace.

What is spiritually correct for you?

Relationships

Relationships by design push our emotional
buttons toward healing, if we are willing.

RELATIONSHIPS INVOLVE INTERACTIONS THAT provide us with schoolhouses full of lessons, which help us define who we are in the world. Without relationships, we cannot grow beyond our earlier mishaps. Short and long-lived relationships all have lessons to teach us about what is important to us and what we need to learn to continue to grow beyond old thought processes. Most people want to start by examining their relationships with others. Let's start this exploration with the person you interact with every day—yourself.

Self Reflection

A RELATIONSHIP WITH YOUR true self is a top priority en route to a meaningful existence. It establishes how you relate to others. Perhaps more importantly, it helps other people understand how you want to be related to. Relationships between others and ourselves are the bread in our lives. The types of grains we harvest and prepare for baking will determine the density and nourishment of our bread.

In this book's Dedication, I thanked my ego for wanting to protect me, for being my so-called "protective soldier" for decades. However, the day came when I wanted to try new things. My desire was to thrive and walk freely into a new life, believing that my possibilities were endless! I could no longer let my ego continue to control my life. Its fear held me back from taking myself to more bread-and-butter opportunities on a higher spiritual journey. Realizing the ego is a necessary part of me, I promised not to kill or squash it in my personal growth process. I encouraged my ego to come along and see its new place in our life by telling it, "I love and appreciate you." It was time for my ego to trust adult decisions I made, based on what was happening in front of me rather than on sensory perceptions solely from similar past experiences.

Self-esteem is fluid. You can have it at work, but not in personal relationships. You can have it at work one day, and not as much the next day because of something someone said or a moment of defeating self-talk. Varying aspects of your life suffer one day and rebound the next. A relationship with yourself prepares you to love yourself no matter the life condition in front of you.

Explore any fear you may have of a loving relationship with yourself. Why is it difficult for you to love yourself, or at the very least to start to like yourself?

The first road to a loving self-relationship is awareness. A bread baker needs to have the best ingredients. The baker is aware of what is best from studying and practice. Make it a personal daily journey to become extremely kind to yourself. This care is especially important in the worst moments you face.

During a trying time at work, I had made an effort to affirm what I wanted, which was not to have bitter resentful feelings over a position that I felt had earned and had been promised to me but was given to another. I tried to re-express my thoughts and to deny my feelings. That's when I got into trouble. I was snapping at coworkers and loved ones for no apparent reason. I became prone to minor accidents, like knocking over cups of tea and bumping into doorways. To recover, I sat consciously in that grief and cried, even though I was afraid the tears would never stop. Rather than negating my grief and ignoring my fears, the kindest thing I did for myself was to sit in misery. To my surprise, the grief lifted after a mere nine minutes. My ego was calm because I returned to a core belief that UE is in control of the details, that everything is in Divine Order. In my caring for myself, I was able to get to a position that was perfect for my skill sets and better-related to the purpose I try to live within—a position I could not see at the time, but had been there all along and was being prepared for me.

To foster a holistic relationship with yourself, examine your past and current beliefs around the areas causing you the most grief. Let tears fall; they will stop no matter the size of the hurt. Pound your anger out into a journal or beat the air out of a pillow. Pushing fear down creates more opportunities for fear to surface, usually unexpectedly. Looking at a dark emotion shatters its illusion, allowing light to shine through to the real self, not the pretend self we take into the world. I have learned to let fear and hurt emerge quickly so it can easily make its transition, leaving truth clearly visible.

What do you believe about yourself and your worth?

What do you show/do that supports those beliefs?

What causes you emotional pain currently?

What do you tell yourself about that answer?

What do you tell others about your emotional pain?

Is it really true?

List three other ways to look at these situations: one where the other person is wrong; one where you are the victim; and one where you are free from angst. You are the only one who can choose for yourself how to continue.

When I meditate on my view of myself, I see all sides. I don't label the answers good or bad. They are just sides of a complex person. I am courageous, strong, and kind. I am afraid, soft, and mean-spirited. My words sometimes bite people, even though doing so is not often my conscious intention. However, I am grateful that I know how to apologize. UE gives me a gift of understanding people, emotions, what to say, and how to say it to help others. Yet, in haste, I can forget to connect to others and myself. I can get caught up in a mental struggle quickly, easily forgetting that I am—as we all are—divinely protected. I possess self-confidence bred out of love, accomplishment, disappointment, forgiveness, understanding, and continued growth.

What words do you use to describe yourself?

We can all agree that at some time or another in our lives someone has said something that hurt our feelings. Why do words hurt? Is there some place inside us, small or large, that fears the hurtful words are true? Is there a place within that suggests to you that the negative words reveal some part of the real you? And if they *are* true, how can you be lovable? Did the words touch what you believe to be true about you?

Here are some things to ponder:
1. Hurtful words say more about the person talking, than they say about you. Everyone has opinions that are based on their own past experiences or on what someone told them. Those opinions are neither right nor wrong. They are mere statements, and that fact negates their truth in your life and your own experiences.
2. We all have wondrous aspects of ourselves, which is who we really are—our authentic selves. Being true to ourselves allows us to accomplish what we came to earth to do and be who we came here to be. Who you really are is a loving energy; you were born a clean slate of joy and love. The only thing that changed that for you is learned behavior from listening to others—some well-meaning and some not.

3. We all have flaws that make us perfectly human on a journey of self-discovery. Our experiences allow us opportunities to forgive, heal, and help others. We all have a choice to present or not present our authentic self.

Treating yourself with kindness requires compassion. My client—I'll call her Liz—was married to the wrong man for her and held a job that paid the bills, but did not satisfy her creative self. She was unhappy and felt unsure most of the time. I suggested to Liz that she focus on loving herself. She confided that she wasn't sure she even knew how to like herself most days. We developed a plan whereby she began to listen to her self-talk. When you forget where you put an item and call yourself "stupid"—that's self-talk. Cancel the unflattering name calling in your head by turning the meaning around to a kinder sentiment. "I'm tired; therefore, it's easier to forget where I put things." Take time to listen to your self-talk.

Look at the words that you used to describe yourself. Which ones can be changed to produce a kinder statement?

When we desperately want a loving relationship, our true desire is usually to be accepted and to feel happy. Each desire starts within us. If you want to be loved, love yourself first. I'm not talking about the people who say: "I love myself; I buy me whatever I want." Loving yourself is akin to how well you take care of the fundamental aspects of your self-care: Do you brush and floss your teeth daily because you want to avoid hurting yourself with gum disease? Do you eat properly and exercise because it is your way of demonstrating love for who you are? Do you stand up for yourself when someone is bullying you? Understanding you are worthy of good care and acting accordingly is a way to show deep love for the person you are and want to become.

Extreme care and love are not selfish acts. Shall I say it again? Loving yourself does not make you selfish. Self-care is a road map to caring for others. You listen to yourself and satisfy your needs and desires. You feel fulfilled and can thereafter listen freely to others without feeling a grudge or malice which you perceived when you were tired. It is the way to care for yourself and allow you to love others without neediness or control.

What is the most caring thing you have done for
yourself in the last twenty-four hours?

Sometimes there comes a point in your life when you have to face the mirror of your own soul, and realize you can embrace or softly destroy your life: with drugs, alcohol, food, unprotected sex—you pick your poison. We pretend to be grown when we are actually emotionally younger children trying to find our true selves by running astray, getting fired from jobs, overdrinking, or sleeping around aimlessly. Acceptance of where we have come from and who we are frees us to share our stories without making excuses. When we accept ourselves, others cannot successfully belittle us or shame us. Self-acceptance is the freedom you think you will receive from someone else loving you. Without your self-acceptance you are always at the mercy of the other person's view.

With self-acceptance, is it easier to be kind to yourself?
What do you need to accept about your past?
How has it defined you?
Have you forgiven yourself?
Have you forgiven others who were involved?

Joy is an inside job. When we seek it outside of ourselves, it is always fleeting. If the object of your happiness walks out the door and never returns, you let that person leave with your happiness. Your happiness is not dependent upon anything or anyone; it is in you to be experienced at your pleasure, whenever you want to allow it. I am not saying that being in love does not create happiness. It does. I am simply suggesting that it not be your only relationship to happiness.

Internal awareness of happiness exits when things around you are good or not so good. Finding your internal happiness allows you to go to the happy place no matter what external circumstances you are facing. How is that possible? Because you learn through your self-discovery that perceived hard times lead you to greater victories. It's a way to avoid becoming stunted as you live your life.

Parental Relationships

WHEN WE ARE CHILDREN, it is our parents' responsibility to love and accept us as we are, which ensures our best development. But most parents are very busy ensuring that you grow up to be someone they can be proud of with their own parents and friends. Their own uncovered pains and emotional scars can diminish their abilities to parent with the highest and most noble integrity. Just as you have a history that builds the person you present to the world today, your parents have life stories that define them. You need to hear their stories to help you understand how they became the people you see before you. This exchange gives you insight into their past and current behavior. Seeing your parents as individuals outside of parenthood helps you. Without forgiveness, you can choke the life and enjoyment out of both the possibilities in other relationships, and also in your ability to live peacefully in the present moment. Remember: parents aren't perfect, and neither are we.

Forgiveness allows you to move forward; it frees you up to accept and release past hurts. Ultimately, forgiveness is more about you than the other people involved. We forgive to get through and beyond our fears, allowing us to see a reality through less-emotionally tainted lenses. Only you can decide whether to forgive or remain stuck in the past. If you don't forgive, life will create opportunities for you to practice forgiveness repeatedly. Choosing not to forgive feels stifling.

What events repeat themselves in your life?

Forgiveness of family and yourself are critical to sustained happiness. Sit with the idea that parents are human beings capable of mistakes as well as great deeds. Release your parents from the expectations you have of them. That is the most loving gesture you can make to them. Make peace with your past. You get to be free.

Forgiving yourself is a personal gift. Start with your younger self. Understand that when you were a little person, you did the best you could with your little-person resources. Have compassion for that little person that you were. Cry for her (or him). Hold her in your mind's eye and assure her as an emotionally healthier adult that you are in a better place to make a conscious decision to protect her. Ask her to trust you as you are. Try to make a life free of fear and misguided anger.

Forgiveness Steps

1. Take deep cleansing breaths that will open you up to let in your desire to change.

2. List your earliest memories of transgression against you, such as, hurtful words and traumatic deeds under appropriate headings: *Father, Mother, Siblings, Friends, Lovers,* and *Self.* Determine the scars and benefits you have received from the painful times. Starting with your parents is important, because as adults we spend too much time recreating life experiences that give us the opportunity to heal childhood wounds. For example, under the *Father* heading I listed: "He abandoned me at age six, after convincing me during my first five years that I was the apple of his eye." His neglect affected my life in an unconstructive manner—making emotionally

unavailable men very attractive to me for years. I didn't know it at the time, but I was trying to prove to myself that if I were wonderful to a man, then he would stay with me. The benefit of my Father's abandonment taught me to be an attentive parent, making me aware that my actions may affect my children and their behavior.

3. List the feelings you experience as you feel your way through this process.

4. Allow yourself to feel all the emotions that come up for you. Feel gratitude for the benefits you gain. You have to also feel the hurt, pain, and disappointments of your perceived losses. Your goal becomes to accept the events and results created by the trauma.

Forgiveness is not approval of the behavior you either experienced or witnessed. Nor is forgiveness condoning the situation. When you are stuck in "old stuff," "new stuff" has a hard time getting to you. Remind yourself to be compassionate to people who are trying to do their best within their human limitations—people just like you and me.

Lover Relationships

THERE IS POWER IN a connection with other people. Learning to integrate your independent self with the ability to be interdependent is an achievement. Recognize situations in your life that let you know when to lean on and when to be leaned on. You get there through talking and sharing and trusting that the other person finds what you want important in most cases, and not contrary to what she wants for herself. The more you trust yourself, the easier it is to trust others, because even if they let you down, you can trust yourself to recuperate and begin again. The goal becomes finding unity with each other. Your divine connection to others is love. Love is what you give, not what you take. If you are looking for what you can get from the relationship that is not love, rather it is need and dependence on another person to make you feel a certain way. For example, when you are looking for a person with a good job so you can build a financially secure future, recognize that is something different from love. That is fulfilling a perceived need for financial security.

Grown-up relationships are designed to push our unfinished emotional interior. Praise your Ultimate Source that each of us has grown up with some form of dysfunction at some point in our early development years. The past created who we are today. Let this be the day you can embrace it and make a positive change, if it's needed. If you are like me, you can't remember half the things that happened to you growing up. I blanked out that which proved uncomfortable. What I do remember and am now grateful for is my first awareness of pain when my parents argued and later separated, because those times were the start of my praying for wisdom.

A core belief I have carried since childhood is that relationships are hard. I am not good with male-female relationships. Through meditation, I explored why I felt as I did. This is a journal entry examining how I formed that belief over many years:

Deborah, your Dad is never coming back. Expecting a man to love you like your Daddy should have is not going to happen. It's not fair to a partner or to the adult you. The things my Dad didn't know how to do gave me opportunities to do them appropriately in my adult life. For example, I know the importance of apologizing because he could not apologize to others. I know people can love you and not be a part of your everyday life. I've learned fear and revenge damage your life. The longer you fight fear, the greater its hold on you. Look beyond what you see; there are reasons why people respond the way they do. Generally, it has nothing to do with you and everything to do with some previous event in their lives that scarred or colored the way they experience the rest of the world.

Next I confronted my core belief around relationships and how I could come up with a new core belief. Meditation and journaling led me to these new beliefs: Relationships require maturity, emotional honesty (being vulnerable), and acceptance. We don't have to rush to get to know a person. Let a relationship evolve. Listen to your inner self. If there is uneasiness, either stop or proceed with more caution. You can be careful without being fearful. You can trust when it's warranted and retreat when it isn't. Live your life fully; take time to listen to the people you are involved with; and reflect on how you resonate with what others express to you. When a man I was involved with said something I perceived as cruel, the *healed* me could easily ask, "Were you trying to be mean intentionally? Does it give you pleasure to hurt my feelings?" That's my recipe in all relationships: to ask clarifying questions, because to live in fear of losing someone doesn't work for me. The relationship was contingent on my established boundaries. If the man's behavior continually pushed and I had no boundaries, the relationship would not be based on mutual gratification. The directness and sincerity of my questions stopped him in his tracks. Calling him on his behavior gave him an opportunity to think about why he chose a less than sensitive way to interact with me. His explanation told me a lot about where his heart was in the relationship. He said, "I was behaving like a brat because I find myself liking you more than I want to at this time in my life." Ultimately, we realized we were in different emotional places. I had no regret. What I learned from the relationship is: Let's not be reckless or desperate to be in love, nor so carefree with our love that we open ourselves to situations that aren't for our highest good.

Is it easy to love you?

Do you hide your true self, your real feelings,
from the people who try to love you?

Are you allowing the real you to show up in relationships?

> *If you don't show up with your real self, who*
> *are people really in love with?*

Real love is the good stuff: inspirational, supportive, kind, caring, and nurturing. It's our fears and unattended to childhood traumas that are the messy parts of relationships. That pain takes us away from being able to love fully.

In relationships, what you do shows your love better than what you say. When you tell the ones you love what you are going to do without following through, you are diminishing an opportunity to strengthen the love you both share. That disappointment tears down trust and erects walls that begin to block true intimacy. To keep the love emotion strong, you may find it helpful to treat love as an action word. Understand the different ways people feel loved. The exercise below can help you determine what is important to the people who mean the most to you.

> *Ask them: When do they feel most loved? Have them*
> *describe how they know they are loved.*
>
> *Really listen to what they say. Take it in, and vow to find time*
> *and ways to implement what you heard. Summarize what you*
> *heard them say for clarification and complete understanding.*
>
> *Share what you need to feel loved and how you know you are loved.*
> *Be thoughtful and be clear. Show gratitude when you see them trying.*

These are conversations worth having if you are ready to implement the premise of *love* being a verb in your relationship.

We clean up our "old stuff" so that we can love freely and find someone we can really love. There should be no need for "testing" to see if your loved one will still love you even if you treat that person less than well. No more punishing your true love for what someone else did or said to you in years past. Just give and be pure love.

Other Relationships

RELATIONSHIPS WITH OTHERS ARE designed to help us know ourselves better. I had a manager who wrote a critical review of my performance. I was angry and upset because I believed her assessment unfairly ignored my accomplishments, was limited in its scope of my work activities, and betrayed the professional relationship we had developed. My normal mode was to push down my reaction, but the Universe had a lesson in store for me. As I sat at my desk and began to read the review, I felt tears stinging my checks, so I put the memo in my briefcase to read in the privacy of my own home. I couldn't bring myself to read it, so I carried it in my bag for a couple of days. By pushing down the feelings and avoiding reading the memo, I thought I was dealing well with the situation; except I found myself about to cry at crazy times for no apparent reason. I was cranky about any question people would ask. To add injury to insult, I reached into my briefcase to retrieve my calendar and got a paper cut on the knuckle of my ring finger—from the offending document. It was the kind of cut that is slight but hurts intensely for longer than you think it will. My message became clear: It's okay to be in pain and sad about an incident. Mourn it so you can move on.

Think back to a time when you lost something or someone and you thought you would stop breathing. Most of us develop coping skills to get us through the pain of loss early in our life. And because those skills seem to work the first time, we rarely examine those coping mechanisms later in life. We don't ask ourselves if the skills are still relevant, and therefore we forget that we can make different choices. What worked for your seven-year-old little self cannot protect your adult self. We need new skills for a new decade.

The coping skills you develop as a young person within your family may not serve you well in your adult relationships. Your habitual behavior probably worked in your family setting, but is often self-destructive when you use it to cope as an adult. You try to recreate what you experienced as a child because you believe you survived fairly well in that environment. The authentic parts of ourselves that we put away as children to avoid being judged want to come out and be healed in our adulthood. When you try to deny those feelings and desires, they show up in your life regularly to help you acknowledge and accept all aspects of yourself.

My client was stuck in behavior adopted in her childhood that wasn't helping her be successful as an adult. She would shut down emotionally when she couldn't figure out how to have disagreements. She would become overwhelmed by the enormity of emotional investment required for successful relationships.

I recommended she sit with the discomfort and ask herself questions. I guaranteed her that her fears could not exist when she shed light on them. One morning she woke up to underlying feelings of dread for no apparent reason. She was happy and fine when she went to sleep the night before and slept soundly all night. Unable to shake off the looming feelings, she sat quietly by herself and said good morning to the emotion.

"What do you want me to know?" she said to her emotions.

Her immediate thought was; "Acknowledge that I'm here, don't push emotions away."

"What do you stem from?" she asked, having learned it is helpful to name the emotion.

"Fear," the emotion answered.

"Fear of what exactly?" she asked, wondering where this exercise would lead her.

"Does it matter?" Her emotion responded with attitude.

"I suppose not." she responded, because her goal was to make friends with her emotions by being agreeable.

"Okay, I'll make room for you. Welcome to my morning." She thought as she settled back.

In that moment of acceptance, she heard, "Fear I'll never be truly loved."

That startled her, because in reality her family and friends loved her. She was dating men who were attentive, open, and kind, and she loved herself unabashedly. She found the courage to ask, "What does *truly loved* look like?"

"It's someone who loves you for who you are with all your flaws," she heard her emotions say with less attitude and more sincerity.

My client told me she worried that she was weak for wanting to be in a committed relationship, because her little girl coping skill was to berate herself for wanting a relationship. Her rationale was: If she didn't need anyone, then no one could hurt her. Tears flowed from that small question: What does *truly loved* look like?

My client chose to examine her feelings in order to be free of her past beliefs about relationships. She reported sitting with the dread for a few moments and allowing the feeling to evaporate in what turned out to be less than five minutes. If she had pushed it down and had gone about her normal routine, negative feelings would have reared their heads throughout the day, causing her to act out by snapping angrily at innocent people.

She knew this because for years she had those encounters and could not explain why. Making a conscious choice to use her Free Will to enrich her experiences, to examine her life and her choices, took her closer to seeing a life plan without fear.

What is your definition of unconditional love?

How does it feel to love yourself unconditionally?

How does it feel to be loved without condition?

Be prepared for quiet and sometimes not-so-quiet discontent. It is normal to feel afraid and agitated when we are on the brink of a new place in our thoughts. When the old pattern of relating to others doesn't suit us anymore, we have to be open to viewing a larger life for ourselves. Personal evolution is expansive, scary, rewarding, and exciting, all of which is integral to living a full life with yourself and others.

Taking responsibility for your life is an adult decision. Some people have said it's easier to give others their power; then they don't have to be wrong. People who allow others to control them can blame those others when things go awry. They have become comfortable with being victims.

The other issue with this method is it's an immature approach. When we are children, others tell us what to do, because they have experiences that give them knowledge that children do not have. However, once you have grown up, it's time to make your own decisions, time to learn your own lessons. No one can grow for you. Letting another person determine what you will learn and experience keeps your existence small and unaware. You can decide to stay stuck, but you cannot reach your full or partial potential. Stop your ego from keeping you away from your dreams.

The definition of *ego* has changed over the years. When I was a young person, people with egos were defined as those having an exaggerated sense of self. They had an insatiable need to be seen and heard, or to out-do other people's accomplishments. Today people understand ego to be that internal voice that guides you away from your authentic self, leading you to base decisions on past and limiting experiences. People create experiences that prove their original premise. If you think every love relationship will end like the first one, you will do things to ensure that happens. Then you can say, "See, I knew it would turn out poorly." Proving yourself right, even though the end result hurts and is not what you really want, becomes the order of your life. You have the power that can stop the madness an ego can create.

The ego is a loving yet fearful expression in your life. The ego is never satisfied. You buy a beautiful ring, and shortly after you walk out of the jewelry store, it looses its appeal. You like it, but it didn't give you a sense of long-term fulfillment. You can substitute for the ring any purchase or external chase you have ever decided to go after. Notice how you feel after you acquire what you have pursued.

How long were you excited by the acquisition?

When did the happy feeling leave you?

Did it last as long as you thought it would?

Will the "next thing" create the fulfillment you are craving?

Accept that you have an ego, but don't let it rule you any longer. The ego is the voice that makes you believe in *if only* ... if only I had the right house, furniture, car, or love, then I would be happy. Then I would be okay and everyone would see my worth.

The ego believes you are separate and alone, with something to prove. Here's the real deal: No matter what you accumulate externally, it never satisfies the soul. The authentic self is always enough. Your soul knows you are worthy of all things and wants you to become aware of it. "What's the difference?" you ask. If you have nothing and can be joyful with nothing to prove to anyone, you are free to be you. You accept all aspects of yourself and understand why you are who you are. You don't struggle with others' opinions because you accept them for where they are: people on their journeys; and you expect them to do the same for you. If they can't, then "Oh well" becomes your best response.

The ego is not bad. It exists to protect us. The problem with its protection is it keeps us from enjoying the journey toward new accomplishments and is happy to help us stay emotionally stuck. Traumas in childhood (alcoholics in the family, a controlling caregiver, mean sibling behavior, sexual, verbal, emotional abuses, or scolding teachers) create the ego. Your traumatized little self decides how it will act to handle the trauma. Ego helps you put on a personality mask and you begin to believe the way you act is just who you are. This sets up patterns that follow you; people say things or do things that require your mask. Take a moment and list what you complain about that others do or don't do.

What do the complaints have in common?

(Those are the areas that your soul is asking you to pay attention to.)

What do others close to you complain about in your behavior?

What do those complaints have in common?

The ego is posed to whisper to you that people always do that to you, because you aren't good enough, because you are an imposter. When you get (fill in the blank), people will treat you better. Then others will recognize you have made it. Again, it is not true. No matter what you acquire, the ego is not designed to be satisfied. It keeps you busy looking for solace outside yourself. Yet, the solace can come only from recognition of what the soul wants, which seems like a risk, but is really the very best life has to offer for you.

Early in our lives, between one and five years old, we create beliefs that become the rules that we live by. We spend our adult lives reinforcing those beliefs as true. Those beliefs are our pattern of thoughts; when life is unexamined, what we do is just habit. Don't let the fear of intimacy tear your relationships apart. The scary thing is, the more intimate we are with others, the better they see our flaws, those that we have been so diligently denying and repressing. These very ideas create a fear inside us; some of us begin creating walls. When asked about it, we pretend we don't know what the other person is talking about, which creates more separation. Emotional truthfulness is a requirement for close and intimate and rewarding relationships. Isn't that what we are all hoping to share with the people we love?

What does the relationship need? Each relationship has *your* need, the *other person's* need, and the need of the *relationship*. Different people look for different things to feel loved. I encourage you to understand what is important to you and why it's important, and to seek the same information from the people who mean the most to you. You learn about yourself and the people in your life. Seek to understand:

What do your loved ones need to feel loved?

What are you willing to do to help loved ones feel loved?

Your answers are a conversation worth having with the people you care most about in this world. Let people describe how they know they are loved. Really listen to what they say. Take it in, and vow to find time and ways to implement what you heard. As you share what you need to feel loved, show gratitude when you see them trying. You may not get everything you describe as quickly as you would like, so focus on what you do receive that is close. Share your gratitude for each thing you see. What you concentrate on is what grows in your life. Concentrating on what you are not getting magnifies the very thing you do not want.

We started working with our relationships with ourselves to enrich the ways in which we are able to interact with others. Relationships create richer lives. As we come to know ourselves well, we can stop fearing that if we lose someone, we won't be able to continue to live. The fear of people leaving us (abandonment) is a natural fear for most people. We can more easily navigate that kind of loss when we know ourselves well. We can hurt, we can heal, and we can learn what works and what does not. That knowledge makes us better for all the other relationships to come. We all want love, so we might as well begin understanding what love means to us.

Love is the good stuff: softness, beauty, kindness, caring and nurturing. Our fears and unattended childhood trauma are the messy parts that take us away from being able to love fully. Clean up your stuff so you can love freely and be with people you can really love. We all have a choice whether to present our authentic self. For those who don't agree with making a choice as an option, think of no change as a choice for your relationships. To speak from your authentic self is the will of your highest self. Grounded in your truth, only you can know for yourself. No one can tell you who your best self is. You find authenticity in the silence of your own heart. We want love, and we must feel safe giving and receiving it. Love is our natural state of being. Love, like nature, is primarily cooperation.

Free Will and Divine Order

Accepting Divine Will as my course of action freed me to experience profound love and joy on a consistent basis.

YOUR BREAD IS BAKED and ready to be sliced. You have *Free Will* to slice it as you see fit—straight or even, some slices thick and some thin. Or you can surrender to Divine Order and be led to feed yourself and others with the bread.

What if Ultimate Source wants only the best for us and lets us define it through Free Will?

That question would suggest each of us is capable of accomplishing or denying any or all aspects of our lives. This premise would allow us to be limited or advanced by what we believe. I imagine that the Designer of Free Will does not take pleasure or pain in our human acts. If any Supreme Source did involve itself, it would be an emotional wreck, laughing with glee one second, and reverberating with tears and horror the next moment.

Could giving us Free Will allow Ultimate Source to be impartial to our shortcomings?

We perceive life to be precious because it is short-lived. In contrast, isn't it possible that Ultimate Source's eternity may be far superior to what we experience in our short lives? Eternity grants all the time there is for us to get the life of our desire.

Free will is powerful because it gives us the freedom to think any way we choose. Your thoughts put your life into motion as much as your movements do; in fact, you can't have movement without having a thought first.

What correlation do you see between where you are
in your life and its creation via your thoughts?

Examine where you are in your life. List the areas of gratitude and happiness. Also list every problem, worry, and discord that is related to your current perception. Take the next two minutes to blame everyone else for your problems. Now that you have that out of your system, define for yourself what role you played in each interaction.

How do you choose to use your Free Will?

As long as there is breath in you, you can change your circumstance. Put your thoughts on a mental chalkboard for review. Take a deep breath and hold the thought that emerges. Is it a supportive thought? Could you write it twenty-five times and feel good about it each time? If the answer is no, don't just erase it; remember from grade school: You can still see the words no matter how faint on the chalkboard. Wash the board clean with loving replacement thoughts that make you proud to be you. You have Free Will, which translates to: You have a choice to change your thoughts at any given moment.

As an adult going about your life, you are causing and hopefully learning from life's experiences. Use your ability and Free Will to change your life for the better. Start by finding the parts of you that people forgot to notice and love. Listing those parts of you is critical to your self-journey toward your authentic self. Your authentic self is your healed self. When you heal the hurts of years past by means of replacement thoughts, you are free to feel and be who you choose to be in the moment. Making decisions in the moment is a part of what it means to live in the moment. You make automatic decisions on how to react from your past. Your reactions may have nothing to do with current reality because the past clouds your thoughts. When you show the world your authentic self, you will find most people admire your confidence. People will admire you, not because you need or even seek the admiration, but because the energy you exude will be pure. Some people may still dislike you and try to treat you poorly. But you will realize two things: Their dislike says more about them and where they are in their journey. Also, on your journey, you have healed the old notion of being less than wonderful. You have discovered your worthiness and can see it in others, whether they see it or not.

What thoughts do you think regularly that do
not serve you in a positive manner?

Your purposeful thoughts are your connection to living a passion-filled life. Your purpose is to recognize this connection. Our purpose gives our lives meaning and happiness. You have Free Will to accept the purpose for your life. Once you accept Free Will, you can take the next step to surrender to the understanding that Ultimate Source loves us and never forsakes us. It is Ultimate Source's great pleasure to give us the desires of our heart—most likely, the desires Ultimate Source put there when we were born. So no longer is it necessary to fight Divine Order for our greatness.

I sat in meditation with this question in mind for several weeks. *What is my purpose? What am I here on earth to do?* The question filled my head and heart because at the time I wasn't happy at work, with no apparent way out. I was tired of being afraid that God's way would mean a boring life for me. I was ready for the meaning in my life to be defined. The answer came from my heart, and I heard it clearly in my head: "Inspire and educate."

My first reaction was a joyful, calm feeling. My second reaction was an audible, "Oh no, I have to go back to college to become a teacher." That did not feel good within my heart, nor within my wallet, because teachers are not paid enough. I began to journal, trying to understand what it would mean to my life to inspire and educate people. Within a week, I read an article about life coaches helping people identify and reach the next level in their lives. I could do that, I thought. After all, I had been doing it with friends and coworkers most of the time for years. It's what I did for free most days—inspire people to be all they wanted to be. I helped educate them on new ways to think about their lives. There were countless times I had no idea what I had said to someone; yet they would come to me and say, "You have no idea how you inspired me when you said ..." That was how I knew it was a message to keep doing what I was born to do. The people and circumstances show up regularly. I am honored to open myself up to what the Universe wants me to accomplish.

I am not vested in what the person I work with decides. My vocation requires that I listen carefully, ask penetrating questions, and say what I am moved to say. Today people pay me to coach and support them toward more fulfilling lives. No matter how tired I am, I always have energy to talk to others. That's how I know I am on track with my purpose. This book is another attempt to inspire more people to be all they were delivered on earth to be.

What compliments do you receive repeatedly?

What do you do that makes time seem to fly by?

What are you doing toward your destiny for personal greatness?

When we surrender to Ultimate Source's will, we make space in our life for what is supposed to be, and we can call that Divine Order in our life. In this context let's consider Divine Order and your purpose to be synonymous. You will be guided; you will feel peaceful and brilliant when you do what you are put here to do. Your purpose doesn't have to be a global or a national movement to be your purpose. It is merely that thing that serves others and gives you an inner knowledge that you are where you were meant to be. It is paying attention to how you feel and knowing that it is right for you. If you accept Ultimate Source's Will as the best that can happen no matter what it looks like, you experience freedom. When you accept Ultimate Source's Will for the very best that life has to offer you, you lose the need to question: "Why me?"

For most of us, surrender feels like giving up. For years I fought being an author—afraid I couldn't do it well, afraid my life would change too dramatically. I wanted to write, but I held onto two fears. The first was fear of failure. What if my skills weren't good enough? Would it mean *I* wasn't good enough? If that happened, then I would have failed my Source's purpose for my life. How could a perfectionist put herself out there to be judged? And wouldn't it feel like persecution? The second was fear of success. If I succeeded, would I know whether people loved me for myself or for the fame? With success comes travel and being away from my family. Who would I lean on during the lonely nights in hotel rooms?

I surrendered in spite of my fears, and today I gladly give up my self-imposed mind struggles to a force greater than myself. That greatness is Ultimate Source's Will for my life, and I accept it wholeheartedly. That acceptance brought the wall of protection down, which allowed me to see the way to go: coaching and inspiring people's lives, writing books and articles that educate people on ways to find their own connection with the world. It took courage to leave self-imposed fearful thoughts and walk out on faith. The rewards have been pure joy. After a coaching session I am elated. After writing a perfect sentence I am smiling. My core is delighted, and that glow follows me around for hours, affecting my interactions with others in the most positive sense.

If God is the Greatness that put us on earth, as a descendant of Greatness, do we inherit that type of DNA? Our Free Will gives us the ability to accept, deny, or just ignore this concept. Turning our backs on our own Greatness doesn't make us less; the reality is no matter what behavior we display to the world, our worth and greatness is our truth. The Ultimate Source can have infinite patience with us because Source already knows the truth of who we are.

My desire to write surfaced when I was a freshman in college. I could have created opportunities from throughout my twenties and thirties but was too afraid. I started writing earnestly in my forties. When I finally decided to face the fear by doing what I feared the most, Ultimate Source gave me ideas. For years I could not spell well. I was the original person to be grateful for spell check. Once I started writing and trusting my voice, spelling came easier to me.

We can begin again at any time we choose. We can look into the mirror deep into our soul and make another choice. Freedom lies in the power of choice, which is always a personal activity. The mind thinks yes I will or no I won't. In the blink of an eye, we can begin to see life differently than we did a mere second ago.

Our being here on earth sets our intrinsic worth. Our decisions magnify our lives or diminish our light. But neither is attached to our worth, because Greatness is in us!

Free will is our choice. We can prosper or flounder—our choice. Universal Energy will back your choice. The cocreation process becomes easier when you open yourself up to Ultimate Source's Will. Free will gives us the cocreative aspect of living. The subconscious mind supports your beliefs and decisions.

Are you free enough to disagree with conventional thinking?

Freedom starts within the mind; choosing freedom is a decisive moment that can lead to self-acceptance and empowerment.

Have you freed your mind to believe what you know to be true for you?

Surrendering to an idea of something greater than you depends on your ability to trust the natural order of things. It requires you to have complete trust in the wisdom of the Ultimate Source's Will, which created all that is in existence. You stop trying to direct your situation because surrendering relieves you of your need to control. Your daily mantra becomes "I surrender to Ultimate Source's Will in my life," because you trust that your Ultimate Source knows better than you what you need. Surrender becomes your way of acknowledging that your faith is stronger than your need to make something happen. Surrendering says I don't need to know why I haven't received the desire of my heart today. Rather, you learn to appreciate the divine plan for your life is in perfect order. Surrender creates peace between your heart and mind, which allows you to say, "If my situation does not change immediately, I remain grateful for God's Will that permeates my life."

Acceptance requires you to trust your ability to rise to the occasions presented to you, while surrender requires you to trust in the divine. In acceptance, we acknowledge we are feeling lonely, hurt, forgotten, or tired. In surrender, we release fear, pain, and sadness no matter the length of time it has been with us, because we acknowledge Divine Order is at work. If your desire is meant to be in your life, it will arrive at just the right minute, when you choose to allow its existence. This thinking may feel passive to people who need to be in control. You can broaden your circle of friends, change routines, and ask for what you want, because surrender is a peaceful knowing that your desires will be fulfilled even if you do not know when or how Ultimate Source will handle the details. Ultimate Source made us wondrous. When babies are born, people love them because they are a clean slate. We refer to the miracle of life. That feeling of possibility begins to change as the child grows and forms its own personality. Where did the wondrous go? It is still living inside the child, and therefore also in you and me. It is in the child's imagination, laugh, art—whatever the child does well. The wonder is in your gift to the world around you.

I am told I am a great listener. Because it comes so easy to me, I assumed everyone could do it. Not everyone does, so when I listen deeply and hear what a client is (and sometimes what they are not) saying, we both learn from the conversation. I use my listening skills to help question clients so they can identify what is important in their lives. A person who lives their life on purpose is choosing Free Will and Divine Order for their best reality.

Surrendering to Divine Will meant I agreed to the purpose for my life. I'm here to inspire others. Once I surrendered, I could accept all the things that came easily to me and use them to create a life of meaning that I can be proud of accomplishing.

Before I surrendered, I wanted to be a writer for nearly thirty years. I would write and judge my work harshly. It was not good. I could not find my voice. I tried to write like other successful authors that I admired, and the writing had not worked. When I leaned into and surrendered to my purpose, my voice became strong and clear. Words flowed from my authentic self. Opportunities to write came from the thin air. People would tell me they were moved to tears after reading my words. When the Universe saw I was serious about doing what I came here to do, I felt supported in ways I could not have guessed or imagined.

There is a plethora of books on the power of positive thinking and manifesting the desires of your heart. Cocreation is easiest when you are clear about who you are and what you want. Add your feelings to what you want to create. Feel as if it already exists. And watch what comes your way. Detach from the outcome, trusting that the right thing is coming to you. Be amazed at how close the outcome is to your vision of what you wanted to cocreate. Be clear about what you want. If you are not sure or if it is not materializing, stop and ask yourself a few questions.

What are you afraid of if you get the desires of your heart?
What will you lose?
What will you gain?

Let go, and know you can never predict the future. Free yourself, and be responsible as you make decisions about your life. Connect with your disappointment and suffering, not blaming or asking "why me," but facing it. Don't run from the problem. Stay in the feeling to let it completely transform you. Real transformation happens when you get to the core of who you are. Your truths, your wants, your disappointments and your shortcomings must be acknowledged as much as your greatness. Your greatest challenge lies in your greatest transformation, often jump-started by a seeming tragedy. You can decide to lift yourself from where you are. You can emerge powerfully to accomplish what you want. Step into your purpose. I see myself as a cocreator when I am functioning at my highest vibration.

There was a time when I would struggle with the idea – am I in control of my life or is a Divine Source in control? I couldn't decide which path to follow. I would struggle with Divine Order around relationships, but lean on it for deciding how to fulfill my purpose. The compartments in my life had to become integrated and be lived in the present moment. I had to find a peace with cocreation or Free Will. Back to basics I went: meditating and journaling through various levels of understanding at different times. Thoughts came to mind, like: What if we live at various levels of emotional awareness throughout our lives? At different levels we depend on brute force or mere coercion to make things happen. What if we decide to cocreate what we want in this life, and what if we begin to grow while trusting a Divine Source? It's as if we are a part of that Source just like a bucket of water is part of the ocean we took it from.

How can the idea of Divine Order help you?

Explore if there are any similarities with Divine Order and your desires. Divine Order guides us toward our peaceful and brilliant self. Divine Order is a beacon filled with ideas and movements we access when we are calm. When we are anxious our ego can push us to believe we must make something – anything happen. When we are aligned with Divine Order our intention and activities create a life worth living.

Deciding that the Divine Order is wise and caring freed me to trust that which I can't see. There is energy in love and acceptance that allows me to believe that no matter what happens, I don't have to judge it. The worst that can happen teaches me about myself and opens up new avenues to pursue.

Living from the Heart

When you can look at success and failure with the
same value, you can have a divine opportunity to learn
more about yourself and others around you.

L IVING FROM YOUR HEART is the setup for the sweet taste of butter in your life. Living from your heart and knowing how worthy you are stretches you beyond old wounds to allow you to love more deeply and openly. Love for yourself and others involves incorporating into your heart decisions you once made strictly from your head. The work you did in chapters one through three prepared you to make decisions that are easier to manage, because they set the stage for you to become emotionally more mature as you resolve old hurts. That maturity allows you to live in the present moment, judging what is happening to you based on how you feel in the current moment, no longer based on recycled emotions from what happened to you in the past.

I have a client who remembers family stories of being an energetic and happy person until he was four years old. That's when he started noticing how unfair things were in his parents' household, with one set of rules for his father, a stern, patriarchal figure, and another more controlled set of rules for the people in the home perceived to be weaker—his mother and the children in the household. It became easier for him to hide all emotions so his controlling father could not know if his manipulations were penetrating. It took months of questions and answers and his digging deep beyond the surface of his feelings for the client to realize he had two emotional ranges as an adult. He either felt fine or he felt extreme anger, which he could reach within seconds in a conversation. No one in his family could determine when his mood would change. That dark anger would cover his face, creating a stone-cold stare that could stay with him for days.

At the beginning of our conversations he could not accept his family's assertions that they were afraid to have heartfelt conversations with him. His outburst and subsequent shutdown made open dialogue too difficult to attempt.

Many philosophers say there are only two emotions: love and its opposite, fear. All other emotional labels can fit one of those two. Keep asking yourself why you feel the way you do until you can get to the bottom of your emotion (love or fear). List the emotions you have had in the last week. Think of as many you can remember: joy, sadness, and so forth.

1.
2.
3.
4.
5.
6.
7.
8.
9.
10.
11.
12.

How does each emotion fit within the love or fear label?

Are there any emotions you could not categorize?

For those emotions you cannot identify as love or fear, describe what was happening when you felt the emotion. Was the event love-filled or fear-based? What did it remind you of from your past? These are the types of questions that can help you dig deeper toward uncovering your early emotional habits so you can decide what your authentic response is to be in the present moment.

We establish emotional behaviors early in our lives to help us survive. These patterns may benefit from examination, particularly when used in adult relationships that are not working. I am an advocate for emotional maturity, our ability to manage our emotions and adapt in ways that honor our spirits as well as the person we are interacting with. When we understand how we affect another person with our words and deeds, and thereby convey that we value that person's uniqueness, we establish a basis for positive connection with that person.

Being aware of your emotions can help you decide if there is going to be butter available for your bread; otherwise, it is likely day old bread that you are serving to the world. Be mindful of how you feel throughout the day and night in your various surroundings. Keep a log listing time, location, and emotions. For example, a journal entry may read:

> I was talking to my good friend, and she said something hurtful. I am feeling upset. My language is in the gutter, and my reaction to this person is quick and harsh. I felt myself in an exaggerated state and asked myself, "Why am I so upset? What does this remind me of? Is this situation different from that past memory?"

After writing your entry, step back, listen to yourself, and then evaluate. After some practice, you will become truly self-aware in mere seconds, which allows you to stay in the conversation with little to no internal interruption or shutting down. This is being present with the person you are talking to as well as the encounter. Being self-aware allows you to be in the moment and fearless.

When people say hurtful things, you are able, with your new awareness, to ask questions from a clear heart. With no animosity, you can ask, "Are you trying to be hurtful?" Or you can decide not to say anything, realizing the person you are talking to is coming at you from that one's own past experience. That is not an excuse for poor behavior; it is a compassionate realization. Compassion comes from your heart, and empathy puts you in another person's shoes.

Living from the heart is frightening to many people. Consider this to be where the stirring of the butter begins. A basic fear most people have is of losing love. We all know people who find it easy to look for love but never get the love they deserve. That fear-based void feels safer than actualizing the true desires of your heart, going after everything but the one thing you have wanted since you were a young dreamer. This is the time you begin putting everything you have learned about yourself in the pot and watch the churning process. Now is where you begin to realize that you want to be loved with all your fine points and all your flaws. It is when you accept and love yourself. A heart wants to be loved. Fear can keep us from receiving the love we so richly deserve.

Loving yourself allows you to see clearly. You identify what feels right within your heart, and you get filled up to do what you were sent here to do. When that isn't happening, when you are feeling split into two people, when you are happy only in someone else's presence, don't confuse those feelings with living from your heart. That is really living from fear and a failure to look deeply into your heart, where your true essence is waiting to be acknowledged.

The questions get harder in the upcoming sections because you will be digging deeper into the real you. Do not fear, because the better you know yourself, the more you can trust yourself to hear what is true for you.

Why is it acceptable to hide your heart's desire and merely exist rather than attempting to live out loud and express your heart's desire?

Discussions from your heart are more meaningful to the people you talk to. If you are talking to others while having thoughts about getting your point across so they will think you are smart or right, you are not speaking from your heart. When we plot what we will say before the other person finishes his or her thought, we are not having a powerful conversation. Heartfelt conversations focus on understanding how the other person feels about what is happening or being discussed. When you focus on getting your point across, you focus on your ego, rather than engaging with the other person. Our ego makes us believe that we are feeling safe and in control. When our ego is in charge, our authentic heart is harder to hear. That's why the Universe sends us little whispers from our "real desire." When we listen, a state of openness begins to shift in our hearts. Listening with your heart is non-judgmental. Amazingly, the connection created creates an environment of true understanding.

Can you imagine what it would feel like to detach from an outcome that you put your heart into?

What did you learn about yourself upon detaching from an outcome with your last conversation?

Our emotional awareness is important; it allows us to react freely from our heart space. When we are aware we can identify, assess and decide the appropriate response in the moment, which helps our personal growth. Growing into our best self requires that we be gentle with ourselves. Our emotions don't cripple us when we choose to perceive and integrate them toward our desired life.

Your power comes from understanding yourself, accepting yourself and being confident in your abilities. Your positive sense of the person you want to be is your real authority. However when your opinion of yourself is formed by past experiences or what others said to you, don't judge that as either right or wrong. Instead try to allow your opinion to be formed in the present moment; choose conscientiously how you want to feel and process what is happening. That becomes you living more freely from your heart.

One must demonstrate courage to live from their heart because feelings of vulnerability take up residence daily. Many of us want to run away or try to control the situation when we feel uncomfortable. Vulnerability can feel like someone is pricking your heart with tiny pins causing your heart to beat wildly in your chest. Can you sense flight or fight take over your insides? Can you be still and feel the fear? It will pass. Don't react as you always have, instead breathe slowly and feel the fear.

Vulnerability is a part of being human and authentic. It highlights our fears. It is not the predictor of what will happen. It will subside and it will return. It's a part of the fully living condition. It's on the path of fully living with yourself.

We all have flaws that make us perfectly human while traveling on this spiritual journey. Our experiences allow us opportunities to forgive, heal and help others and ourselves. We all have a choice to present our authentic self or not in any situation. For those who don't agree that we have a choice as an option, think of no change as your choice.

Are you gentle or hard on yourself when making a decision?

How does your past influence your present day thinking?

Is there room in your heart to forgive yourself
and others who have hurt you?

Do you have a difficult time choosing to support your desires?

Living from the heart allows us to love with open arms, to feed without expecting to be fed in return from the same person. To love deeply, we remove conditions. Living from the heart, I can love someone and not allow him (or her) to be at the center of my life, particularly if his presence is toxic because he has not chosen to work on his issues. If his idea of loving me is harmful to my spirit and daily being, it becomes prudent for me to let love exist without having to be in his presence. Can you imagine yourself saying to someone you care about:

"I know myself. I am a perfect me, not a perfect person. I know I deserve the very best love. I also know you deserve the very best; if you don't know it, you can't ever receive the best love I have to give."

Many of us prefer not to trust anyone for fear of getting hurt. The heart decides what is right or wrong for each of us. Choices made from an emotionally healthy heart power your decisions in an honest way. Your behavior is a choice; it is a response, not a reaction.

If you had nothing to fear, what would living from
your heart look like in your daily life?

Have you ever experienced living from your heart? Describe how
it made you feel. Was it comfortable or uncomfortable? Why?

We all know commitment-phobic and grouchy people (the two traits not necessarily in the same person). What I am suggesting is people may be afraid of showing their true selves for fear of rejection (the commitment-phobic), which does not mean they do not want to be loved. There are degrees of being commitment challenged. I have known people in long-term relationships who do not choose marriage. And if one partner presses the other they are willing to walk away rather than making the ultimate commitment, not realizing that buying property together and having children bind you anyway.

The grouch doesn't let people get close. The sourness is a covering to keep people at an arm's distance—a form of protection. Remember the earlier chapter on relationships. If and when you ever hear their childhood tragedy it would help you to understand that what you see in front of you is a self-designed bulletproof vest. Think of the heart as the house for soul. The heart is the keeper of your secret desires and the reason you came to the world.

Listening to your heart takes personal courage and belief in the sometimes illogical. You find your authenticity in the silence of your own heart. Your heart may tell you to leave your job and attain a graduate degree with no extra money in the bank.

A friend in her late thirties could not justify the desire of her heart, which was to go to law school. She attended graduate school shortly after college and received her MBA. However, since she was age thirteen she had wanted a law degree, not to be a lawyer, just for the knowledge. How could she justify a $150,000 education with no desire to work in it every day, she lamented at lunch one day? Intellectually, she understood knowledge is priceless. Knowing that courage can free her to be who she was born to be, I asked her the following questions:

1. Why is it necessary to justify to anyone else the desire of your heart?
2. Do you have dreams of where this additional knowledge can lead you?
3. Are you willing to live with the regret at the end of your career if you do not go back to school?

Living from your heart is the pivotal step toward the smoothest butter; that propels you to give voice to your true self and eases you onto your path of purpose.

You find authenticity in the silence of your own heart. Your authentic self is the will of your highest self. Grounded in your truth, only you can know for yourself what is real for you. No one can tell you what is your authenticity. Life is calling to you to create yourself. Try on personas until you recognize internally: "Oh, this is who I am."

The heart is supersmart. It is who we truly are at the core of our being. The heart has an electromagnetic field that it sends outward. When you truly love yourself and have happiness, your heart's energy attracts energy similar to yours. However, you must be willing to receive it. Scientists have proof that the heart is capable of knowing what is going to happen three to five seconds before you make a conscious choice. Think of the heart as a muscle that you keep open by using it for good, such as by means of service to others that can feed your purpose.

Have you ever volunteered your time to others
who were less fortunate than yourself?
Did you notice you were changed for the better?

I talk to people who admit to feeling better after they help someone else. There is a balance that is required of us. Find your true self and share it with the world.

The Universe wants the desires of your heart fulfilled. Love always wins. It can wash over destruction, it teaches children what is possible, and it forgives where the ego can't. When people point to themselves, they point toward the heart, because there is where we perceive our soul's essence. Our souls remember to love everyone. That is why living from your heart is critical to your survival, creativity, and sanity.

Your Voice and Your Path

Your voice is your responsibility, and your path is your vocation.

LAIMING YOUR RIGHT TO choose the life of your making is the finest bread and butter. The butter is sweetened when you are no longer the victim and no longer merely surviving; because using your voice and choosing your path makes you a thriving success.

It is easiest to use your voice when you have access to your authentic personal power. Only you can know what is right for you. You came to earth with the highest self-goal. That is the direction of your authentic self. No one can tell you what is right for you as an adult. What makes your life and voice authentic is to be the author of your own choices in life. *Authentic* is not what your family, your church, or your culture told you to do. To find your true voice you have to rethink all the beliefs you have been taught and then decide who you are. You may continue to live with those beliefs, but at least you will come to the answers with all the evidence explored.

Who are you, now that you have examined your beliefs?
How do your beliefs help you vocalize what you need?
How do your beliefs hold back your voice?

To engage your voice is to make a commitment to bring your best self wherever you are in your day. Take a deep breath, and dare to be you. It is difficult to know who you are, what path you are to travel, and what to stand for when you are fragmented.

There are two extreme behavior types that are worth reviewing. Both use the art of pretending as a basis for hiding our emotional wounds and fears. The first is a person who says what others want to hear for so long you can't be positive where his authentic voice (opinion) begins and ends. The second is seen in people who say and twist words to create chaos and affect others' perceptions. The intent is the same for both extreme behaviors—to keep the light off their practitioners' authentic selves. Both demonstrate a fear to be seen for who they are.

The better you know yourself, the more you can trust yourself to hear what is true for you. Our past experiences help to define us. Unexamined experiences allow us only to react, whereas examined experiences allow us to be aware and make choices about how we will *respond*. Not *react*, mind you; it gives you the power to choose. So how do you find your voice?

1. Define each situation that is important to you.

   For example, you may say, "I must have peace, so I give in to others rather than engage in arguments; that is what is important to me."

   Now is the time to challenge your thinking. Perhaps that is your coping mechanism, not your true feelings. Each situation is different, and some may make sense to ignore, but to ignore all of them is an extreme. Each situation allows you a new choice for your voice.

   If you do not have the luxury of examining a situation in real time, review it before you go to sleep at night. Review your day by asking yourself: What was important? What would you do differently? What were you most proud of about yourself? Go to sleep with a positive thought about you. Tell yourself, "I love me." Self-love butters the hardened places to let your voice come through.

2. What are your boundaries? What can you accept, and what crosses the line? How can you communicate this clearly and without malice?

The first time I had to tell a family member I would not be able to attend a family dinner because I had made other plans was tricky. I had attended many family dinners in the past, but wanted to honor the commitment I had made to another person. I kept my voice steady and calm. I opened with how much I enjoyed our family dinners, and how I was looking forward to others; however, I would not be able to attend the one in question.

I did not respond to the moans and groans. I ended the conversation by saying I understood this was disappointing. I would miss everyone and hoped to see them at another occasion. I was not mean or angry, and I chose not to be pulled into either of those emotions. You guessed it—everyone survived.

Mean what you say and say what you mean. It helps others to accept what is real for you and sets an example for them to follow.

3. How does the conversation or situation add meaning in your life?

If the interaction does not help your life, stop having the conversation or repeating the situation. Going in circles with the same conversation that is going nowhere delivers frustration and continued hurt. If the conversations allow you to see another point of view or to grow, keep having them. Only you can decide what is best for you. It takes practice to be aware enough to do what is best for you.

4. Is your voice (also known as your conviction) taking you toward your desired path, or away from who you are trying to be?

When I started writing, I fretted about whether I would write as well as other published authors. I tried to write like my favorites. As I shared the drafts, I received feedback: "I don't understand what you are saying." "It doesn't sound like you." "It isn't clear." Friends would suggest I write other types of books, like romance novels. It wasn't until I decided to find my own voice that the words began to flow. People began reading my words and reporting back that they were moved to tears. I was on to something. Finally, I no longer had any fear of my own voice.

Self-discovery gives you the strength needed to pursue your conviction. No one has the right to stop you on your journey. Your voice is the tool that propels energy toward your desire. Use it wisely and with reverence to your truth. Malice is destructive and a cover-up that prevents others from seeing what is important to you. It takes personal courage to keep true to your voice. Stand for what is true and important to you, and let the rest go. Start small, and build your voice muscle.

I was ready to be authentic; authenticity is a combination of vulnerability, truth and strength of courage. I know my weaknesses and I know my strengths. I tell the truth about either, and I understand I am still worthy of the very best life has to offer. Bring who you are; bring your real self—not the mask worn to protect some aspect of yourself that was so wounded you decided to cover up with false layers of protection to ensure no one could get that close again. Remember—if no one can get close, no one can really love you. Isn't that sadder than your hurt feelings from when you were five or ten years old, and for some of you, from fifteen or twenty years ago?

Let's look at what it means to be vulnerable, knowing what is happening, and how you react to what is happening around you.

Being present means listening and responding appropriately to someone else. Self-awareness as an idea of being authentic means you strive to be present in each moment. If you aren't present in the moment, you react from old thoughts and feelings. To be present with vulnerability is to acknowledge the rapid heartbeat or sweating palms. It's remembering the bad that happened when you were younger, and still you decide: I am going to react differently because this is a different time, with different circumstances and perhaps different people. Here is where we will feel our feelings, welcoming the dark sides: anger, hate, and boredom, embracing our feelings, and strengthening our voice.

Never be afraid to ask yourself: what can I do differently?

Is there another way to view the situation?

What story am I rehearsing to tell others and myself?

Is the story true?

What are other ways to see the situation?

These questions apply throughout your life, at home and at work and in all relationships. Once you find your voice, it gets easier to ask harder questions that will keep you authentic and aware of your gut intuition. Intuition is your connection to your divine Source, which sends you messages. People recognize intuition in their own way. For some it is a song that comes to mind, a feeling in their stomach that tells them to stop or move forward. Some call theirs a hunch. To recognize your intuition, you want to be alert. You may be racing to a meeting and feeling intuitively that you need to slow down. You don't listen because the meeting seems more important than the hunch. What happened as a result of not slowing down? A slip or fall? The meeting was cancelled, and you stressed yourself for nothing? Or you were the last one to walk into the meeting? Your soul and intuition are as related as your ego and fast pace are.

When others tell you what is best for your life, you can decide to have the courage to trust your own power. You get to choose your definition of success and create scenarios that bring your idea of success forward.

Following your path requires bravery because you must rely on your internal resources to take you to your destiny. You will be met with the wisdom and power you need. Courage met with wisdom and internal powers are forces Superman can't hold back. You can succeed with tenacity and courage; that success provides you with growing wisdom and greater insights.

When you are traveling along your path, don't be disheartened by the chaos that can show up. It is the Universe's way of getting rid of the things that do not serve you well. It can be disconcerting, but this is what I try to remember:

I stay in the moment and identify that which is good: I am breathing. I have people who care about me. In this moment, I am whole and healthy. When I am worried about the future, I am not focused on the present moment. If I am thinking about the past and obsessing about what I should have said or done, likewise, I am not in the present moment. There is misery behind me from my past and worry ahead in my future. The gift of living authentically is in the present moment because then I get a glimpse at clarity. You can name it and you can focus on it.

Asking "Why did this happen?" and "Why me?" keeps us stuck, because there are no satisfying answers to be found. It doesn't matter why bad things happen. What matters is where you direct your sight—is it on the disaster, or the new possibilities? Do you believe there is a director of huge and caring portions, an Ultimate Source, who wants to lead you to your very best and to an ability to help others? Or do you choose to falter and focus on negative thoughts or circumstances?

I was reliving the scene of a car accident I had instead of remembering that my relationship with God surpasses all that appears as negative. The accident was frightening, but I was not hurt. I forgot that the chaos swirls away to create an opening for my good. The accident resulted in my getting a new car of my dreams. It's our choice to focus on trust and not on one's judgment of the negative events in one's life.

Choice is the key to where your focus will land. In each moment, you can stop negative thoughts and think positively. When negative talk begins, ask yourself, "Who told me that?" If it is not your voice, examine carefully whether what you are thinking is true for you. Taking personal responsibility for your thoughts and voice is how you sort through what is right for you.

When you can't see clearly to the next step, stop moving. Pronounce your trust in your Ultimate Source of power. Be still. When the fear and concern subside, ask your highest self for direction. If you are anything like me, you will say things like, "Please be clear, and put it in writing." If your image of your Source is shaking its head from side to side regarding your request, we have a similar imagination.

I always thank the Ultimate Source for answers and then watch as the words come clearly to me, as I am willing to be still and hear them. The answer never intentionally brings harm to another person. It allows me freedom to be the best me. I am best when I am joyful. Joy is quiet and sure. Joy carries me above the ocean's waves so I don't get wet. Joy is an inner peace in the belief that all things work together for ultimate good! Joy is to trust, as peace is to awareness.

Sitting still on my friend's deck, with the sun teasing me between the clouds, I asked the Universe to return me to the joy and peace I have known but misplaced. In that twenty minutes of stillness came a resounding answer in my mind, "Just trust Me. No matter what you are facing, no matter what you have been through—trust that My plan always sees you through!" The ultimate joy is that no matter what worries you have, they disappear when you trust in a Source of Ultimate Power. That trust is powerful; I no longer remember what was upsetting me on that particular sunny day. Notice I did not say "partly cloudy," because I am a "glass half full" person. The Source doesn't turn away from us; we turn away from it or turn toward it. It's our choice.

The value for me in believing in a force that is greater than me is it motivates me to live up to (the bread) and beyond (the butter) what I am here on earth to do. Seeing with intuition and opening up to synchronicity happens when you say to yourself, "I have to do what I am supposed to do with the time I have been given. No more fear, no more procrastinating, and no more excuses. I am here to do the job I was born to do." This belief gives me an internal place to go and be nurtured. When people are cruel, hurtful or indifferent, I have an internal retreat and a prayer to open up my heart and my mind to see differently. It's a place that allows me to grow and learn quickly with less pain. This Source helps me define, and when necessary, *re*define why I'm here and where I can go on my chosen path.

No matter what image you conjure up to the contrary, the false images will fade away. They cannot stay when faced with light. Source's love for you is greater than any love you have experienced as a human being. It is so pure, tears would spring to your eyes at its mercy. You don't have to wait for it—you turn toward it, the way you turn into the sun when it comes out from a cloud on a cool day. The cloud (your fear) obscures the sun (Source), but you must always remember the sun is still in the sky. Trust that Source is still with you when times appear difficult.

Have you been in a situation where your intention or a persistent thought was trying to tell you something and you ignored it?

The road to your path and your voice may not always be pleasant. Change triggers fear and anguish. Just don't stop there—because more of the path awaits you. Get clear on what you want to pursue. Be open to the signs that show your desire is coming to fruition, and trust that the negatives are sure signs that things are moving to get you clear and free of old stuff. The things that are falling apart (relationships, jobs, or possessions) can hold you back or propel you forward.

Journeying on your path may not sit well with someone you know, and that's fine, because it's not his or her path. I travel annually to see my friend at her cottage by the lake. The community is four hours away by car. No one else goes with me. She and I have our own rhythm together. No matter the weather, I carve out an hour or more to take in the lake's sounds, the sun's rays, and the sky's vastness. I write from nature's inspiration because it is my dream to travel to beautiful places to write inspiring messages for anyone who is interested. It feeds my soul and helps others. There is no greater path – even though I travel it alone much of the time.

I can rejoice that I have a wonderfully loving family and the very best friends. Our relationships are full and rich, and our time together is precious. But on this writing path that I have chosen, I need to be with myself to meditate, to write, to edit, and to reflect. When I stood up for my vocation, some people had to fall by the side of the path. The ones who loved me most understood and embraced my decision with enthusiasm and encouragement. You want to be clear about your dreams before embarking on your true path.

Remember we are here to grow. Each one of us has a choice to grow or stay put. We have fears and concerns, and yet they are our teachers, if we decide to learn and move into a well-lived life. That's the best butter on your bread.

Which choices in your life are you most proud of?
Which choices in your life have caused you pain?
Which choices in your life have you abdicated to others?

Your choices define who you were in that moment when you made them. With each moment, you can decide to choose wisely, based on all you have learned about yourself and what your voice tells you is right for you.

I had a young client tell me that the problem with listening to himself was he told himself wrong things, and therefore made wrong decisions. When he stopped listening to others and started taking responsibility for what he decided to do, it became easier for him to see what was right. He now lives a life of making choices that are right for him and his young family.

You determine what is right for you and allow your voice to support your choices. If your soul's plan is to help you discover the real meaning of the life you planned before you were born, the key to understanding your soul's plan is listening to your heart, voicing your decision, and using personal courage to enact the plan. When we take personal responsibility for our lives, our real joy is tapped. As long as you wait for someone to decide your fate or for something to bring you joy, it will elude you.

Happiness is dependent on external factors. Someone giving you a gift brings happiness, or buying yourself a new car, but how long are you happy? You may be happy for a moment, but joy can last a lifetime because you can pull it up from inside you. Joy is internal and fills voids when not everything around you supports you. Your voice and your path are your birth's plan. When we do what we came to do, we are usually in service to others. Those we serve can learn by our example or by our assistance.

Possibilities and Potential

There is excitement in possibilities.

B ELIEVING IN A PRESENCE of something greater than my power opens up grander possibilities in my heart and belief system. Understanding there is an energy that created the solar system, allows flowers to grow out of cracks in the cement and the miracle of birth gives me a sense of potential. We are told in physics that energy exists in everything. It cannot be created or destroyed – it just is. Energy can be transferred between forms. Energy causes molecules to vibrate. Potential energy is a force like gravity. A ball thrown up in the air will stop in mid-air and then begin falling to the ground. Its kinetic (in movement) transformed into potential energy (we know it will land in the future moment). This Universe is energy; a force that flows through all things. I do not pretend to understand all the theories of physics. I do believe however in the power of energy in this world of ours. That belief allows me to know there is a force (I call it God, you may call it something else) that can tie possibilities together for our greater good.

Can you open to all possibilities with a unified mind and heart?

It's our choice to be receptive to limitless opportunities for extraordinary living.

We are designed to live with potential that is within our reach. One's potential is rarely achieved sitting in front of the television. A person who lives his truth and shares it with others without expectations is living with a purpose. That purpose is a balance between love and service. It allows you to create a life full of potential and in concert with your Ultimate Source.

Finding your vocation should be aligned with your purpose whether big or small. In our twenties, it is often the thing we are most afraid of tackling, because we are not terrific at it the first time we try, or someone told us we couldn't pay the bills with that vocation. You may have presented a thought or feeling and someone judged it harshly.

Was that the first time you chose to pull back and
not show all of you for fear of disapproval?
Did someone tell you your desire is unacceptable,
and did that statement shut you down?

In our thirties, we become so good at excuses we begin to bury the desire as a youthful dream laid to rest. Often by our forties we become aware of what is not working and ready to commit to looking back for those desires of our youth.

When did you first realize people judge the real you?

Ultimate Source's love for me is larger than my flaws. That Source sees past my indiscretions to love me beyond my wildest imagination. In the early morning light, I lie in the serenity of Ultimate Source's grace. My breath is as effortless as a bird's serenade. In the quiet, I remember Ultimate Source provides for me a purpose as assuredly as I believe the bird's purpose is to provide song. I seek the direction of that purpose in my meditation and check in with my feelings throughout the day. I give thanks for the territory covered this day and ask for the courage to continue the course tomorrow. My path is cleared of debris, my heart is open, my eyes are hopeful, and I am mindful. The day ends with a powerful peace in my sleep.

The Universe is fine with us having more of anything and everything—more love, joy, and prosperity. We can stop putting limits on ourselves and declare more of what we desire.

Give your Ultimate Source permission to help you hear what is possible—your desire, or something better than you can imagine. When we do the work of our Maker, we feel in sync with our connection to Source, to others and to the world.

My soul dwells in the energy of a God as the Source of all things, the Creator of beauty and truth. I am divinely scripted in my time of need. This assured calmness blankets my ego and emotions, creating space to hear and not judge; see and not fear; love and not destroy; laugh and denounce sadness. My confidence and poise in every situation grows out of my faith in Universal Source to take me to greater heights! I am not dismayed when a job promotion doesn't come my way. It was not mine to have; the Universe is better than I am at creating Divine Order in every situation. I am not diminished when a lover leaves. He was not mine to have; the Universe has a better plan and a more loving mate in mind. I am not destroyed by the appearance of disease. Eternity and miracles are natural and promised. These beliefs create all the possibility I can handle.

To know your own personal truth is to own your power. Living in the awareness of possibilities opens the door to messages. To embrace possibility and potential requires courage. Power is the ability to influence and change ideas. When we work for the collective good, we can influence the outcome of events. Just remember: power can't be delegated without your consent.

To what degree do you let energy of possibility loose in your life?

What do you wish would come true in your life?

Why do you want this?

How would your life change if you got your wish?

Does the answer still frighten you?

Who do you need to forgive, or what do
you need to heal to get past fear?

Are you willing to give up everything in your current
life to have this new possibility come true?

Do you have to give up?

What are the compromises?

If you choose to stay where you are, can you
find peace with that decision?

We have discovered throughout this book that thoughtful answers come when we dig deeper than the surface. When you define your root cause, you can stand firmly and achieve something more meaningful for yourself and those you choose to surround yourself with.

I listen carefully to my Source when I want to evoke potential. "I've got you," God says to me in my meditation. "The details are preordained."

I entered a contest put on by a local store. I declared myself a winner, and I knew I would be at the moment I put the card in the bowl, because I felt a connection to the future. The possibility connected with my senses to create the reality before it happened. For an instant, I was transformed. Two weeks later I received confirmation of what I already knew. I won the contest.

The journey continues daily; Ultimate Source will take care of the details from your thoughts and energy. Therefore, commit to living, not just existing. The Ultimate Source is open to taking care of us; be certain, and have unwavering faith in Its potential. Why is unwavering faith recommended? Because we are using our Free Will to believe in a truth that is a light to freedom.

God never forsakes us in our time of crisis. God is within us. Leaning on God's Source helps me become a cocreator with God in my life. We get to choose to turn toward or away from our Ultimate Source.

What is your choice?

We don't have to try to force what will happen any longer. Relax into it and rejoice when whatever comes rests upon you. Ultimate Source is at the center of all potential. It is our cocreator of abundance.

For years, as I would listen to successful people talk about how their lives unfolded, I would cry, without understanding why my heart was so touched. I would weep when I saw people who actualized their dreams and their preordained destinies. Those tears were the beginning of living my own potential. Just suppose before we are born all the many possibilities for our lives are laid in front of us and appear throughout our lives as nagging desires. Our soul remembers the possibilities that the Ultimate Source has in store for us. And why are so many of us afraid of those possibilities? Often, when we are young, we can't express where the desire emanates from, so it's easier as we grow to turn our backs and say it's a pipe dream going nowhere. Examining why I cry helped me understand that God gives me tears for others to encourage me to extend a helping hand. My insights helped me to stop the sorrow and start writing. Now I understand that my tears for successful people, myself included, are not only for the challenges of realizing our desires, but also for the sheer joy of seeing our possibilities come true.

What goal have you been too busy to go after?
Would the Source of all things want to restrict whom
you are and what you want to accomplish?

Your possibility for a delightful, potent, and fulfilled life is your choice! Design what you desire with a grateful heart, awareness, and acknowledgement of your Ultimate Source. Stand back and watch the miracles unfold. I will stand with you and wish for unlimited bread and sweet butter for the rest of your life.

I often wonder why we stay the ill-fitting course for far too long. I have read that some psychologists believe people commit to a failing course of action because they are trying to be right. People will stay on a destructive course, like eating too much, not eating enough, drinking too much, not exercising enough, or venting too much anger, longer than they should, even if it is doomed, because they want to justify their original decision. It is as if people are trapped mentally in an unsatisfied path. People feel as if examining what they believe and how it makes them feel is too difficult, because examination will show they are wrong—what they thought and continue to believe is wrong. And if they are wrong, then their foundation is shaken.

Here's what to do: Stop for a moment. Accept yourself where you are now. Think: "This has been me." Become willing to be the you who is now open to change based on an authentic and thoughtful you. Be willing to examine your thoughts, beliefs, and emotions for the new goal, which you get to establish.

There is also a secret *sin* (which means here to miss the mark). People are unwilling to change course and be authentic because they never truly feel "good enough." They hold on to the bravado or shyness (two sides of the same thing—hiding their true self) no matter what their accomplishments or lack thereof, because they secretly say to themselves, "If people knew the real me they would never accept me." Remember this journey is a self-discovery.

The other secret very few people know is when you show your authentic, loving self, people are drawn to you in unexplainable ways. People who do not care for you leave you alone for two reasons. First, like bullies, it is no longer fun to harass someone whose button they can't push. Second, they tend to respect the real you even if they do not like you. The better news, the creamy butter oozing off the bread here, is you become compassionate and less judgmental. When that happens, you no longer worry about what others have to say.

Decide which path you are on that you may want to veer away from. Ask yourself:

> *What reasons do you give for continuing down the path*
> *that does not serve you well? (Is your answer positive or*
> *negative? Do you feel uplifted or on a downward spiral?)*
>
> *How much more time do you plan to give this course of action?*
>
> *What are the reasons you should stop?*
>
> *What can you do to replace what isn't working for you?*
>
> *Are you willing to shift your way of looking at this?*
>
> *(List situations that may be causing issues.)*

When you are stuck in your thinking, start to move. Do something to move the energy within you around. Dance, exercise, do yoga, or walk. Be watchful for new ideas or feelings about what to do to move your situation.

A life coach listens to people intently to understand where they are in their development. One of the things I have noticed is intellectual processing, answering questions with the right answers. Clarifying becomes very important; control and perfection are important to people who know they want changes but aren't ready yet to really move. They usually set aside the emotional side. You know they are there and you think you are in control. But are you really?

Try this exercise: What do you want most in life? Write about what it would feel like if you had support for what you want most in life. Describe what your emotions would feel like. Feel the emotions you described. Every time you feel down, bring the strong, positive emotions back. Make those feelings your support system. Supply for yourself the emotional support you had been seeking from outside sources. Move slowly and take small steps. Stop telling the naysayers in your life what you are hoping to accomplish. Share your dreams with those who support you. Keep your focus on the good feelings you created.

List your accomplishments from the last twelve months. Include changes you made, new things you tried, and times when you generally felt good about yourself. If you can't think of anything, look at previous months on your calendar. Who did you help last year? Put what you recall on your list. If you don't have any accomplishments begin the business of creating situations you can be proud to report.

These are the building steps toward creating more possibilities. Awareness of how your steps build success gives you more confidence. As you get stronger in your abilities, you can branch out to new things. Ideas are plentiful, and you have the foundation to know which ones to try and which ones to turn your back on. When you try things that don't work, you now have the foundation to speak your truth and move on.

Are you a hero in your own life?

Are you proud of the energy you have put into the world?

If your answer is yes, how can you be of service to others so they too can live their possibilities? If your answer is no, what is holding you back? *Do not blame anyone else!* Start with yourself.

What do you tell yourself that is still holding you back?

Is what you are telling yourself really true?

What did you do to contribute this?

Have you done this before?

Why are you repeating patterns that do not serve you well?

How do you ensure you don't do this again?
What lessons can you learn, and what change
can you incorporate into your life?

What thoughts are you carrying that hold you back? Thoughts can change, grow, and transform, or thoughts can shrink you and put you in despair. If we attach to random thoughts that create suffering, we become stuck. Assess that which is personal to create a foundation on which to build new possibilities.

Examine your thoughts with courage, so you can choose to be a hero in your own life. Whatever you accept as true for you, remain kind to yourself. Be gentle with yourself; it will spill over into your relationships and create the energy of love. The Universal Energy can expand possibilities and potential when you are on board.

Faith in something grander than myself carries me through every aspect of my life. You have identified what you are able to lean on and believe in. Those beliefs need to be positive enough to take you beyond your imagination into possibility. Your potential honors what is important to you. It allows you to learn something new that brings you joy. Potential can excite you.

Joy is a spiritual union between life's unsettling moments and knowing you are divinely protected. Joy understands that what is happening around you is real, but it does not define you. Joy is a quality that resides in each of us, one that rides with us through the negative stuff in life. Joy is an energy that allows us to see beyond problems to the potential for better. Joy is a faith in something greater than us. Joy reminds us that we have moved beyond hard times before and survived, often in a better way than we could have imagined.

When I was in my thirties, I moved to a big city where I had a handful of work acquaintances and fewer real friends. After I paid bills, I would have no money left for fun activities, which gave me time alone to get to know myself and to define what was important to me. Surprisingly, after the loneliness subsided in those wintry days and nights, I found that internal joy began to keep me company. I found that path to joy when I realized our perils are always temporary. No storm lasts forever. In fact, a storm will blow over, but many of us keep it alive in our thoughts. The decision to keep talking about what happened weighs us down. We are human; therefore we feel sadness, hurt, and pain. It is our choice to stay in those feelings or to find our joy in the possibility and potential of what lies ahead.

What makes you smile that has nothing to do with anyone else?

What do you like about yourself?

What do you dislike about yourself?

How can acceptance of both free you to see beyond where you are today?

What is something you can give to another with no expectation of anything in return? (Giving with no expectation can produce unexpected joy.)

If you watch television, listen to the radio, or read newspapers, you have seen that these media are fraught with tales of victimization, cruelty, and violence. You can make a conscious decision to be different. You must know that the opposite of what you see and hear is possible. As each of us shines a brighter light, our collective energy begins to shine brighter. That light is energized by joy. Choosing joy, no matter what is in front of or behind us, is a courageous act. I tell clients often: this is your life and therefore your choice.

When you understand the importance of choosing your reactions, life no longer happens to you.

A client was laid off three weeks ago. She organized a support group of other laid-off people. They share leads, review each other's resumes, and help each other with mock interviews to engage potential employers. She volunteers and talks to people about the possibilities she is looking to create. She has two positions that are larger in scope than what she was doing. One offering was for a job below her skill, which she shared with a group member more suited for the opportunity. The colleague got the job. They chose to look at the outcome they wanted, not the thing that they fear and do not want. They focus on the possibilities.

What are your repetitive thoughts?
Are they what you want or don't want to happen?
What do you believe in, if anything, that is beyond what you can see?
Do you believe anything is possible?
Do you look for signs to support what you want to create, or do you focus on why it can't happen?

By now you have learned that belief in yourself—your confidence—flows around you because you healed pains. You can trust yourself to handle any situation in the present moment. Your confidence doesn't take away from others. It helps you to assume others are as wonderful as you are in their own right.

By now you have seen lots of stuff happen in your life. We can get beat up emotionally, be abused verbally, suffer through jobs that don't suit us, and argue with people we love. We have learned along the way that the secret to good emotional health is to choose our response to the stuff that comes our way rather than allow an automatic reaction to take place. As human beings, choosing involves selecting from a range of options. An automatic reaction occurs when there are unresolved conditions from our past. Choosing is essential to freedom and is accomplished through emotional health and awareness.

Hopefully, you have learned which serves you better: peace or resentment. Have you heard people say they have a right to be resentful of the people who did bad things to them in the past? Have you also noticed how unhappy they seem to be? Peace is health, wholeness, and awareness. Furthermore, you do not have to take on someone else's issue as your own. (For instance, from a boss who verbally attacks your idea with unwarranted aggressiveness.) We all make mistakes; forgiveness is necessary for peaceful living. (As when someone you love and who loves you acts out of step with love and more in fear.) All situations appear different without anger or resentments. (Displaying anger toward a neighbor whose party was too loud inflames all subsequent interactions. However, without anger the next encounter is a civil and often pleasant exchange.) The stuff of life demands we become aware of our responses to ensure we grow stronger and more peaceful.

The clearer we are, the easier it is to make our dreams a reality. Those dreams are the table where we sit with our bread and butter, which make possibility and potential nurturing and sustaining elements in our hopes and desires. These are the things that make our lives grow in the most amazing ways. This, ladies and gentlemen, is the bread and butter of life! Peace be unto you!

Additional Life Discovery Questions

THE LIST OF QUESTIONS below is to help you continue to grow into the person you are meant to be and present to the world. Some questions may be perfect for where you are today, while others may make more sense to you years later. One way to ensure you don't age negatively is to keep growing. Find things that interest you, and always include yourself on the list to learn new things. Look at various sides of a question. Think like a debater; take up the argument of the other side of the question. You may be surprised where new thoughts can take you. Ask yourself empowering questions. If your right question is not here, let these inspire you to ask the questions of your heart.

Who told you to believe … (*insert a belief you have never questioned*)?

Is there room for another theory about that belief?

Are you angry about what happened or something else?

What is your highest calling? (Define your purpose)

What gives you energy? What else?

What are you most afraid of doing?

If you were to find out you had three days to live, what would you do?

If you were to find out you had three months to live, what would you do with your days and nights?

If you were to find out you had three years to live, what would you do with your last three years?

What holds you back from doing the things on your list?

Are you hooked on feeling powerless?

How do you feel after you have procrastinated?

Are those the feelings you wanted to have?

What kind of man or woman do you want to be?

How does your fear hold you back?

How do your excuses hold you back from accomplishing what you want to do?

Who are you if you don't do what your heart wants you to do?

If you were the author of your life, who would you be?

If you rethink all that you have been taught, who would you be?

What are the unlimited possibilities that you have not thought of?

What is the most transformation you can create for yourself?

Can you see your greatest challenge as your greatest possibility for transformation?

How can you be of service?

What is the secret of your joyfulness?

Do you believe you can do the thing that you have been putting off?

How have you grown since last year?

What is different about your life this year from last year?

Have you deferred your dreams another year?

How long are you willing to defer pursuit of your dreams?

What part did you play in things not working out with someone you care about?

Is it easy to love you?

Do you hide your true self, your real feelings from the people who try to love you?

Are you allowing the real you to show up in relationships?

What beliefs are between you and that which you really want to have?

Do you believe you can achieve your desire?

Do you have a plan?

Where is there an opportunity for you to do something meaningful?

How can you help others?

What were your childhood talents?

What guilt, if any, do you feel about your early family members? Think about each member you knew or did not know: your father, mother, siblings, grandparents, childhood friends, guardians …

If you are more successful than either of your parents or siblings, does your success hurt them?

Did anyone tell you while growing up you were too smart? Not smart enough? What messages did you hear that you still carry around with you?

What do you want most in life?

Who can you help?

What do you do better than most people?

Your Notes

Your Notes

Your Notes

Your Notes

Your Notes

Reference Books Read and Recommended by the Author

Erroneous Zones	Dr. Wayne Dwyer
Seat of the Soul	Gary Zukav
A New Life	Eckhart Tolle
The Art of Power	Thich Nhat Hanh
The Four Agreements	Don Miguel Ruiz
The Mastery of Love	Don Miguel Ruiz
the power of receiving	Amanda Owen
Blissology: the Art & Science of Happiness	Andy Baggot
Women, Food, and God	Geneen Roth
The Artist Way	Julia Cameron
Quantum Wellness	Katy Freston
Trust Your Vibes at Work	Sonia Choquette
Go Put Your Strengths to Work	Marcus Buckingham
How To See and Read Aura	Ted Andrews
What Happy People Know	Baker & Stauth
Extraordinary Relationships	Roberta Gilbert MD
The Answer is Simple	Sonia Choquette
Trust Your Vibes	Sonia Choquette
The Tao of Physics	Fritof Capra

In the Flow of Life	Eric Butterworth
The Instruction	Ainslie MacLeod
Excuses Be Gone	Dr. Wayne Dwyer
The Abundance Book	John Randolph Price
The Edgar Cayce Primer	Herbert B. Puryear
Unity: A Quest for Truth	Eric Butterworth
Real Magic	Dr. Wayne Dwyer
Meeting faith	Faith Adiele
Synchronicity: The Inner Path of Leadership	Joseph Jaworski

About the Author

DEBORAH LIVERETT IS A certified life coach and a senior vice president in corporate America. For the last eighteen years she has made a concerted effort to live her purpose, which is to teach and inspire willing people put in her path. Since beginning her career as a human resources professional in the early 1980s, she has helped countless people, both personally and professionally. In 2002, she moved into corporate philanthropy. She made every career change with the intention of helping people discover their potential and passion for living life extremely well. She has been a lecturer, instructor, and coleader of Women in Leadership forums, vice president of a professional development committee, a global philanthropic grant maker, and mentor. Ms. Liverett was a contributing on-line columnist. She wrote Motivational Moments for several years. She is a graduate of the Coach Training Alliance. Ms. Liverett's company is called LiveLifeCoaching. She is the proud mother of two sons and three grandchildren. She resides in Chicago and this is her first book.

CPSIA information can be obtained at www.ICGtesting.com
Printed in the USA
LVOW12s1042191114

414351LV00004B/4/P